The W[illegible] Highla[illegible] White Terrier

Barbara Hands

John Bartholomew & Son Limited
Edinburgh and London

The Publisher wishes to thank The Kennel Club and The American Kennel Club for permission to reproduce the breed standards.

First published in Great Britain 1977 by
JOHN BARTHOLOMEW & SON LIMITED
12 Duncan Street, Edinburgh EH9 1TA
And at 216 High Street, Bromley BR1 1PW

ISBN 0 7028 1074 6

1st edition

Prepared for the Publisher by Youé & Spooner Ltd. with illustrations by Barbara Hands and Malcolm Ward

Contents

Preface

The Westie is one of those canine extroverts whose belief in its own importance in the scheme of things can only provoke amused admiration. Being a tough, hardy little dog of a sensible size and structure, the Westie has climbed rapidly in the popularity charts and is a firm favourite with the pet owning public. The author of this book has many talents, not only being a successful breeder and exhibitor but also a writer and artist who can convey her knowledge of the breed in both words and pictures. All the jaunty charm of the West Highland White comes through with lots of practical advice on ownership, both for those who are looking for a cheerful companion and for those whose ambitions lie in the direction of exhibiting and breeding.

Wendy Boorer
Consultant Editor

Introduction

The Westie is one of a number of terriers originating in Scotland and is very like the Cairn Terrier. Indeed until about 1917 the two breeds tended to be mixed, the Cairn breeder using the occasional Westie. This can be seen in early pedigrees, some Cairns having Westies in their pedigrees and the same dogs appearing in the pure Westie pedigree. The well known Harviestoun line of Cairns included Westies in their pedigrees. One example of this was Ch Morven (Westie) appearing in the pedigree of Harviestoun Raider (Cairn).

It was thought that originally the white puppies were 'sports' in a litter of coloured terriers. They were unwanted and destroyed. It was Colonel E.D. Malcolm of Poltalloch who realised how easy it was to mistake one of his brown terriers for vermin – and shoot at it. From then on he decided to breed only white dogs and it is Colonel Malcolm who can be given the credit for the beginnings of the breed we know today.

From this beginning we can see the character of the Westie. The dog was a hunter, fearless, and tremendously self-determined. It had to be small and strongly built to enable it to do a day's work in the very rugged landscape of the Highlands. It had large strong teeth to enable it to kill vermin and a double weatherproof coat to keep it warm in the most inclement of Northern climates.

This then was the origin of the West Highland White Terrier. Consequently, although it is small and cute as a pup, it must be firmly handled (because of its instincts) to get the most from it and to make it become socially acceptable. As it is in the Westie's temperament to chase and kill vermin it must be taught from a very early age that the fluffy tabby from next door does not come into this category.

The word terrier comes from the Latin word *terra* which means earth, and this betrays another trait of the Westie. There is nothing the dog likes better, when out for a walk in the woods and fields, than to start grubbing about in earth banks and piles of leaves. It is inquisitive by nature and loves to explore. Unfortunately to a dog there is little difference between a grassy bank in the woods and a lawn or small patch neatly planted with rows of colourful flowers.

From this we can see that the Westie is not designed to be a lap dog. It is a small, game, hardy terrier with a geat deal of self-determination.

If you accept this then the Westie is 'the best dog in the world'. Easily trained and intelligent, it is equally at home in town or country. Very adaptable, the Westie loves to be part of everything you do and hates being left at home. It is faithful and loves to be with its master.

Westie c. 1900 and Westie c. 1970

POINTS OF THE WEST HIGHLAND WHITE TERRIER

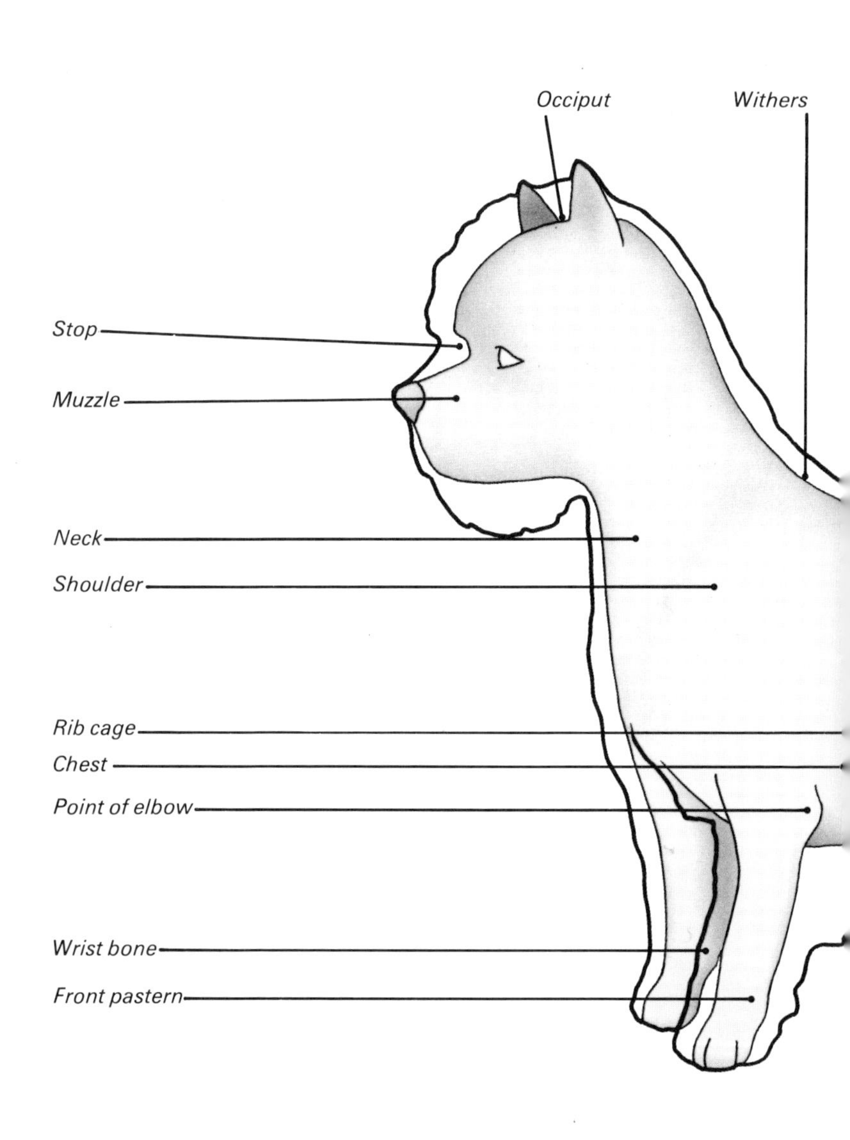

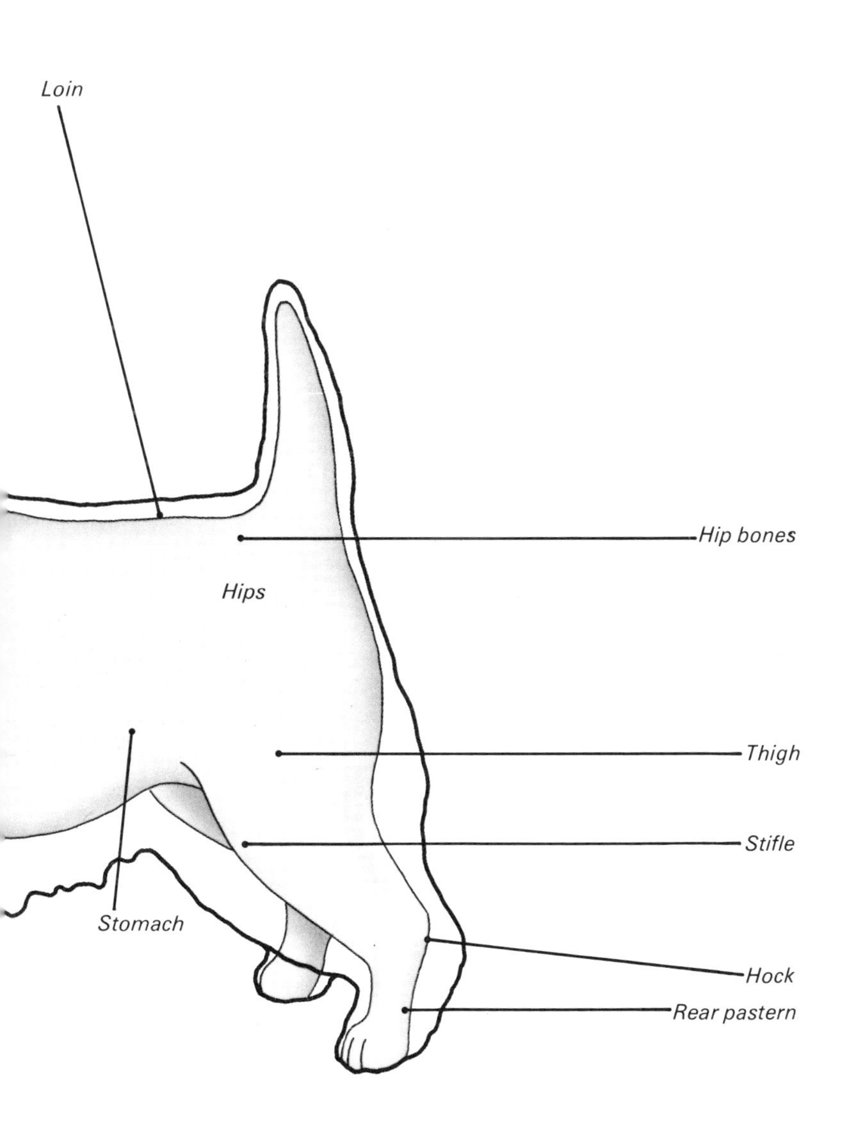
Loin
Hip bones
Hips
Thigh
Stifle
Stomach
Hock
Rear pastern

The breed standard

The British Breed Standard

General Appearance *The general appearance of the West Highland White Terrier is that of a small, game, hardy-looking Terrier, possessed of no small amount of self-esteem, with a varminty appearance, strongly built, deep in chest and back ribs, level back and powerful quarters on muscular legs, and exhibiting in a marked degree a great combination of strength and activity. Movement should be free, straight and easy all round. In front, the legs should be freely extended forward by the shoulder. The hind movement should be free, strong and close. The hocks should be freely flexed and drawn close in under the body, so that when moving off the foot the body is pushed forward with some force. Stiff, stilted movement behind is very objectionable.*

Head and Skull *The skull should be slightly domed and when gripped across the forehead should present a smooth contour. There should be only a very slight tapering from the skull at the level of the ears to the eyes. The distance from the occiput to the eyes should be slightly greater than the length of the foreface. The head should be thickly coated with hair and carried at a right angle or less to the axis of the neck. On no account should the head be carried in the extended position. The foreface should gradually taper from the eye to the muzzle. There should be a distinct stop formed by heavy, bony ridges, immediately above and slightly overhanging the eye, and a slight indentation between the eyes. The foreface should not dish or fall away quickly below the eyes where it should be well made up. The jaws should be strong and level. The nose must be black, should be fairly large, and forming a smooth contour with the rest of the muzzle. The nose must not project forward giving rise to a snipy appearance.*

Eyes *Should be widely set apart, medium in size, as dark as possible in colour, slightly sunk in head, sharp and intelligent, which, looking from under the heavy eyebrows, imparts a piercing look. Full or light coloured eyes are objectionable.*

Ears *Small, erect, and carried firmly, terminating in a sharp point. The hair on them should be short, smooth (velvety) and should not be cut. The ears should be free from any fringe at the top. Round pointed, broad, large and thick ears are very objectionable, also ears too heavily coated with hair.*

Mouth *Should be as broad between the canine teeth as is consistent with the sharp varminty expression required. The teeth should be large for the size of the dog, and should articulate in the following manner: the lower canines should lock in front of the upper canines. There should be six teeth between the canines of the upper and lower incisors. The upper incisors should slightly overlap the lower incisors, the inner side of the upper incisors being in contact with the outer side of the lower incisors. There should be no appreciable space between the incisors when the mouth is closed, ensuring a keen bite; a dead level mouth is not a fault.*
Neck *Should be sufficiently long to allow the proper set on of head required, muscular and gradually thickening towards the base, allowing the neck to merge into nicely sloping shoulders, thus giving freedom of movement.*
Forequarters *The shoulders should be sloped backwards. The shoulder blades should be broad and lie close to the chest wall. The joint formed by the shoulder blade and upper arm should be placed forward, on account of the obliquity of the shoulder blades, bringing the elbows well in, and allowing the foreleg to move freely, parallel to the axis of the body, like the pendulum of a clock. Forelegs should be short and muscular, straight and thickly covered with short hard hair.*
Body *Compact. Back level, loins broad and strong. The chest should be deep and the ribs well arched in the upper half, presenting a flattish side appearance. The back ribs should be of considerable depth and the distance from the last rib of the quarters as short as is compatible with free movement of the body.*
Hindquarters *Strong, muscular and wide across the top. Legs should be short, muscular and sinewy. The thighs very muscular and not too wide apart. The hocks bent and well set in under the body so as to be fairly close to each other when standing, walking or trotting. Cow hocks detract from the general appearance. Straight or weak hocks are undesirable and are a fault.*
Feet *The forefeet are larger than the hind ones, are round, proportionate in size, strong, thickly padded and covered with short hard hair. The hind feet are smaller and thickly padded. The under-surface of the pads of the feet and all nails should be preferably black.*
Tail *5 – 6in. (13-15cm.) long, covered with hard hair, no*

feather, as straight as possible, carried jauntily, not gay nor carried over the back. A long tail is objectionable and on no account should tails be docked.

Coat *Colour pure white, must be double coated. The outer coat consists of hard hair, about 2 in. (5cm.) long, free from any curl. The undercoat, which resembles fur, is short, soft andclose. Open coats are objectionable.*

Colour *Pure white.*

Size *Size about 11in. (28cm.) at the withers.*

Note *Male animals should have two apparently normal testicles fully descended into the scrotum.*

The standard evaluated

The breed standard sets out very precisely what we should be aiming for in the perfect animal. But no-one is ever perfect. However, it is this standard that everyone aims for when breeding a litter, and what every judge has at the back of his mind when judging a class at a show. It should, therefore, be known inside out. Personal interpretations of the breed standard do tend to bring a variation in type.

SKELETON OF THE WEST HIGHLAND WHITE TERRIER

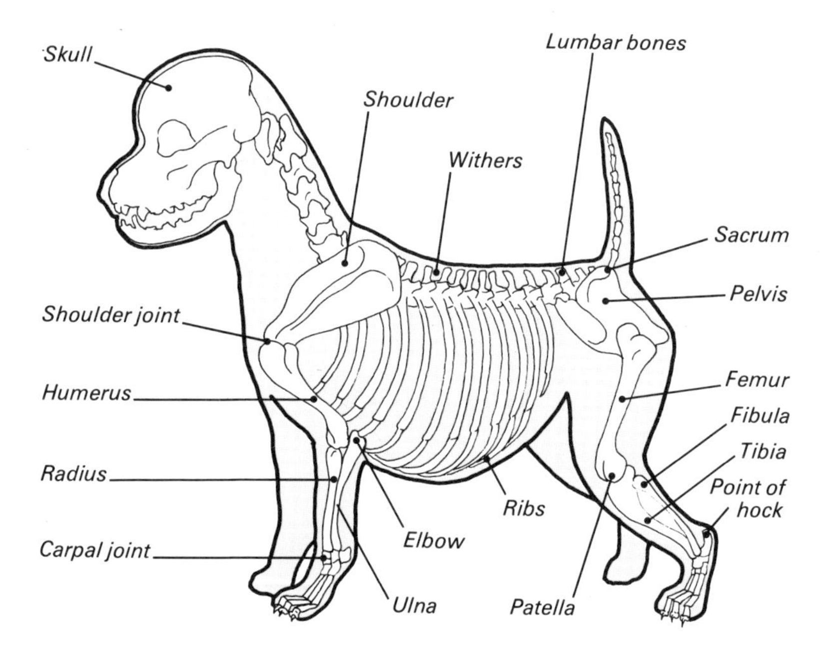

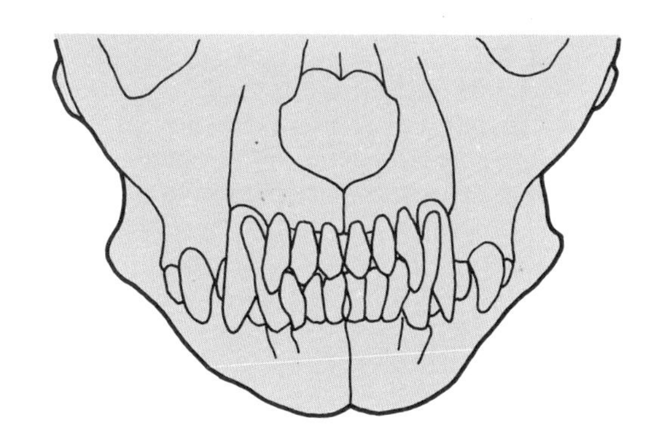

Correct scissor bite

General appearance It should be evident from looking at a well groomed Westie that it thinks much of itself and is full of its own importance. It should be built for work and each point that it possesses should re-inforce this. It should be small and compact with a deep chest and ribs, level back and powerful rear end. The front legs should be straight and strong. The hind legs should be very muscular and strong. The Westie is a medium size terrier and should measure about 11in. (28cm.) at the point of the shoulders. Although no mention is made of weight in the breed standard, dogs usually weigh about 18lb. (8kg.) and bitches a couple of pounds (about 1kg.) lighter.

Head The skull should be strong and well boned. There should be as little taper as possible of the skull from the level of the ears to the eyes. The length of the skull from the back to the level of the eyes should be slightly greater than from the eyes to nose. A long foreface should be avoided at all costs. The piercing look so typical of the Westie is helped by the heavy ridge of bone over the eyes and the slight indentation between them, called the stop. The foreface should not drop away below the eyes. The jaws should be strong. The nose must be black and should form a smooth contour with the rest of the muzzle. If the jaw is narrow and the nose projects, the expression of the Westie is spoilt and becomes snipy.

Eyes Looking from under heavy brows and slightly sunk into the skull, the very dark eyes give that typical sharp and intelligent expression. They should be as dark as possible, but not black, and set widely apart. Without this the expression is completely lost. If the eyes are light in colour or wrongly placed, the dog will not look at you with that piercing expression so typical of the breed.

Ears The correct set of ears is most important to complete the alert, intelligent picture of the Westie. They should be set at either side of the head, unlike those of the Scottish Terrier which are placed on top of the head. They should be upright, carried brightly erect and be as small as possible and sharply pointed. In a mature dog the ears are almost hidden in the head, furnishing which is the Westie's crowning glory.

Mouth The Westie should have what is known as a scissor bite. This refers to the manner in which the teeth lock. The lower canines should lock in front of the upper canines. There should be six teeth (incisors) between the upper and lower canines with the upper incisors locking firmly over the lower ones. The mouth should be broad between the canines and the teeth large for the size of the dog.

Neck and forequarters The neck of the Westie should not be swan-like, but of sufficient length to attain a correct set on of the head – that is at right angles to the neck. It should be muscular and should merge smoothly into the shoulders. This will happen if the shoulder blades are correctly set, a very difficult thing to understand at first until one has felt a truly good pair of shoulders. This is because it is something which must be thought of in three dimensions. First, looking from the side of the dog, the joint formed by the upper arm and the shoulder blade should be placed well forward of the feet and the shoulder blade should be broad and flat. Looking from the front of the dog the forelegs should be straight, short and muscular and set parallel to one another with the elbows tucked well into the sides of the rib cage, thus allowing the correct free pendulum-like movement. It is the proper layback and angulation of shoulders that helps to give the shorter back. There should be no shoulder bulge above the legs but a smooth inward sweep to where the shoulder blades meet and knit into the spine.

Ear carriage

correct

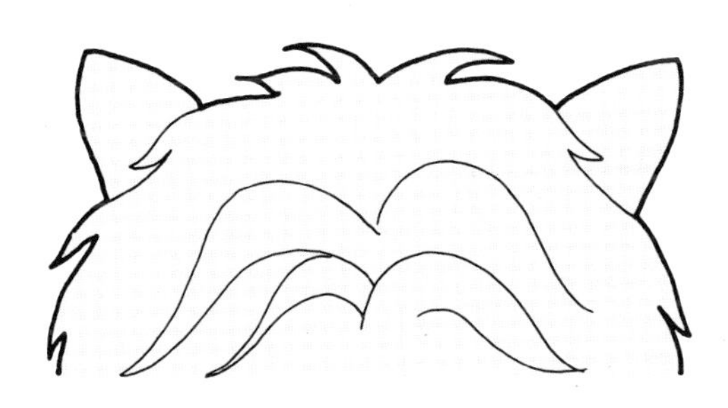

too low

too high

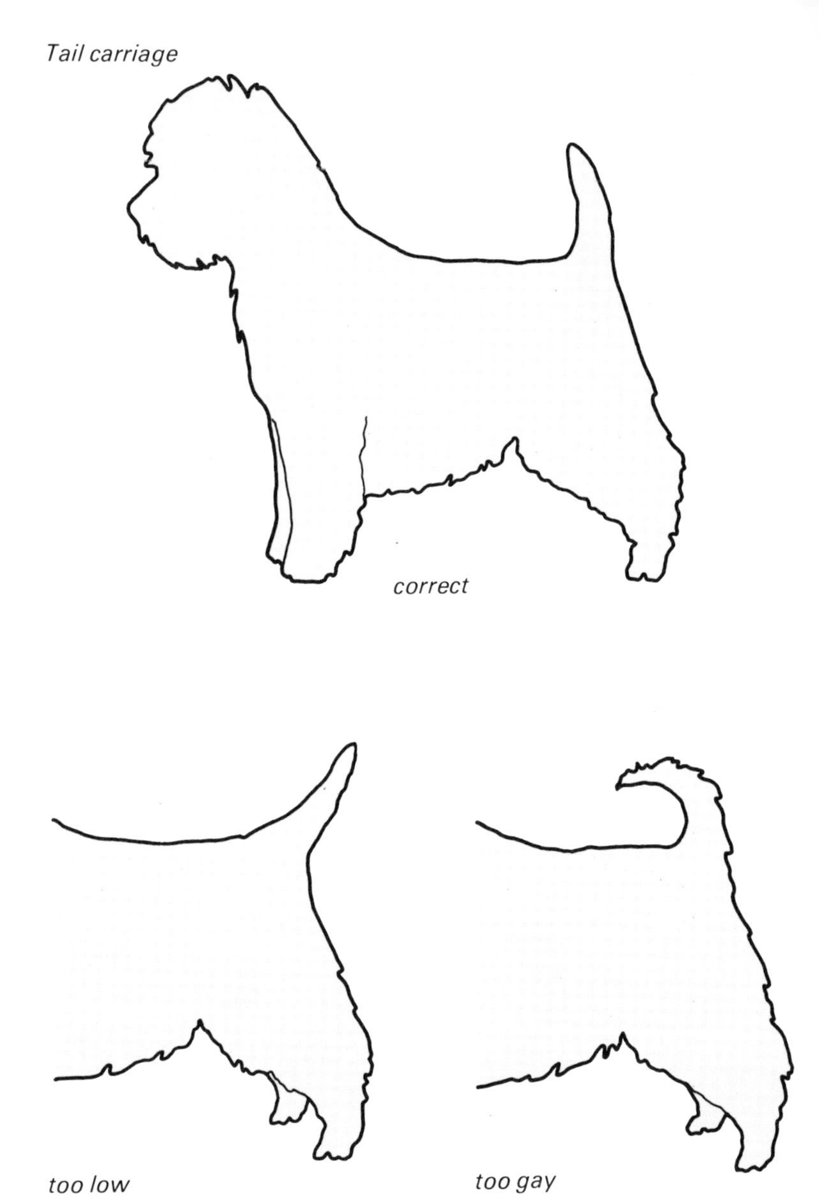

Tail carriage

Body The body should be compact, muscular and level. In the breed standard a short back is not mentioned at all but this is attained with a good layback of the shoulders in combination with the distance from the back rib to the hindquarters being short. Although this shortness is important it must not be so short as to hamper the strong driving movement of the hindquarters. The chest should be deep with the ribs well-arched in the upper half, and the depth of rib continuing right up to the back rib. The body, when viewed from the front, should be flattish and not barrel shaped as in the Scottie.
Hindquarters The hindquarters are strong and muscular, their width across the top making it impossible to see any part forward of them when viewed from the rear. The thighs should be muscular and not too wide apart. The hocks are set well in under the body when viewed from the rear and move parallel past each other when viewed from behind. In movement they should drive the body forward with some force, extending out behind the dog as it covers the ground.
Feet The forefeet are larger than the hindfeet and are round, strong and thickly padded. The pads and all nails should be black if possible.
Tail The breed standard states that the tail should be 5-6in. (13-15cm.) long. However this is the finishing point of the dog and should be in balance with its front half. This usually means that it is about level with the top of the skull between the ears. It should be covered with hard hair with no 'feathers' at the rear, and should be as straight as possible. When moving the tail should be carried jauntily and not carried over the back. On no account should the tail be docked to make it shorter.
Coat This is so important to the overall picture of the Westie but so often wrong. The Westie has two coats, a very soft, dense undercoat resembling fur, and an outer coat, which is longer than the undercoat, and hard and dense. The outer coat should be about 2in. (5cm.) long but this varies in show coats from very short hair on the neck and shoulders to a much longer coat on the body. The outer coat, when seen to perfection, is absolutely straight and can best be described as 'silvery' white – not linty. The soft coats are usually linty white and a dog with the proper coat texture can sometimes look a little grey when seen next to a soft coated dog in the show ring. Sometimes a yellowish strip appears down the dog's back, possibly from the origins of the breed. Some dogs have this

Champion Backmuir Noble James
Date of Birth 9.10.73. Became a Champion Sept. 1976
Owned and Bred by Mr. and Mrs. A. Gellan
Sire of American Champion On Guard of Backmuir
Showing a beautiful head and good front.

Champion Erisort Special Request
Date of Birth 2.7.72. Became a Champion Sept. 1974
Owned and Bred by Mr. K.S. Hodkinson
Showing a short back due to short coupling and a good layback of shoulder.

Arnholme Arrogance of Crinan
Date of birth 2.10.74.
Owned by Mrs. B. Hands
A young dog at the start of his show career. Correctly built but needing to mature fully and grow more jacket to complete the picture.

Champion Candida of Crinan
Date of birth 4.9.72. Became a Champion 4.7.75.
Owned by Mrs. B. Hands
Bred by Mrs. C.H. Clay
The author's favourite.

permanently – in others it will come and go depending on the state of the coat.

The American Breed Standard

General Appearance *The West Highland White Terrier is a small, game, well-balanced, hardy-looking Terrier, exhibiting good showmanship, possessed with no small amount of self-esteem, strongly built, deep in chest and back ribs, straight back and powerful hidnquarters on muscular legs, and exhibiting in marked degree a great combination of strength and activity. The coat should be about 2in. (5cm.) long, white in color, hard, with plenty of soft undercoat. The dog should be neatly presented. Considerable hair should be left around the head to act as a frame for the face to yield a typical Westie expression.*

Color and Pigmentation *Coat should be white, as defined by the breed's name. Nose should be black. Black pigmentation is most desireable on lips, eye-rims, pads of feet, nails and skin.*
Faults: Any coat color other than white, and nose color other than black, are serious faults.

Coat *Very important and seldom seen to perfection; must be double-coated. The outer coat consists of straight hard hair, about 2in. (5cm.) long, with shorter coat on neck and shoulders, properly blended.*
Faults: Any silkiness or tendency to curl is a serious fault, as is an open or single coat.

Size *Dogs should measure about 11in. (28cm.) at the withers, bitches about 1in. (2.5cm.) less.*
Faults: Any specimens much over or under height limits are objectionable.

Skull *Should be fairly broad, being in proportion to his powerful jaw, not too long, slightly domed, and gradually tapering to the eyes. There should be a defined stop, eyebrows heavy.*
Faults: A too long or too narrow skull.

Muzzle *Should be slightly shorter than the skull, powerful and gradually tapering to the nose, which should be large. The jaws should be level and powerful, the teeth well set and large for the size of the dog. There shall be six incisor teeth between the canines of both lower and upper jaws. A tight scissors bite with upper incisors slightly overlapping the lower incisors or level mouth are equally acceptable.*

Faults: Muzzle longer than skull. Teeth much undershot or overshot are a serious faults, as are teeth defective or missing.
Ears *Small, carried tightly erect, set wide apart and terminating in a short point. They must never be cropped. The hair on the ears should be short, smooth and velvety, and trimmed free of fringe at the tips.*
Faults: Round-pointed, drop, broad and large ears are very objectionable, as are mule-ears, ears set too closely together or not held tightly erect.
Eyes *Widely set apart, medium in size, dark in color, slightly sunk in the head, sharp and intelligent. Looking from under heavy eyebrows, they give a piercing look.*
Faults: Too small, too full or light-colored eyes are very objectionable.
Neck *Muscular and nicely set on sloping shoulders.*
Faults: Short neck or too long neck.
Chest *Very deep and extending at least to the elbows, with breadth in proportion to the size of the dog.*
Fault: Shallow Chest.
Body *Compact and of good substance, level back, ribs deep and well arched in the upper half of rib, presenting a flattish side appearance, loins broad and strong, hindquarters strong, muscular, and wide across the top.*
Faults: Long or week back; barrel ribs; high rump.
Legs and Feet *Both forelegs and hind legs should be muscular and relatively short, but with sufficient length to set the dog up so as not to be too close to the ground. The shoulder blades should be well laid back and well knit at the backbone. The chest should be relatively broad, and the front legs spaced apart accordingly. The front legs should be set in under the shoulder blades with definite body overhang before them. The front legs should be reasonably straight and thickly covered with short hard hair. The hind legs should be short and sinewy; the thighs very muscular and not set wide apart, with hocks well bent. The forefeet are larger than the hind ones, are round proportionate in size, strong, thickly padded, and covered with short hard hair; they may be properly turned out a slight amount. The hind feet are smaller and thickly padded.*
Faults: Steep shoulders, loaded shoulders, or out at the elbows. Too light bone. Cowhocks, weak hocks, and lack of angulation. A 'fiddle-front' is a serious fault.
Tail *Relatively short, when standing erect it should never*

extend above the top of the skull. It should be covered with hard hairs, no feather, as straight as possible, carried gaily but not curled over the back. The tail should be set on high enough so that the spine does not slope down to it.The tail must never be docked.
Faults: Tail set too low; tail too long or carried at half mast or over back.
Movement *Should be free, straight and easy all around. In front, the leg should be freely extended forward by the shoulder. The hind movement should be free, strong and fairly close. The hocks should be freely flexed and drawn close under the body; so that when moving off the foot the body is thrown or pushed forward with some force.*
Faults: Stiff, stilty, or too wide movement behind. Lack of reach in front, and or drive behind.
Temperament *Must be alert, gay, courageous and self-reliant, but friendly.*
Faults: Excess timidity or excess pugnacity.

A Westie and two Cairns

Please!

Choosing a puppy

It is so easy to be drawn into buying a puppy by seeing a pretty little white ball of fluff with a very appealing expression staring at you from out of a cage in a shop window. But resist the temptation to buy a puppy on impulse. Remember that with luck that ball of fluff will be your constant companion for many years.

Firstly go to your local library and read as much as you can on your chosen breed. Ask yourself if the character of a terrier fits your way of life and whether you can really cope with a boisterous puppy. If you are very houseproud you are going to suffer torments for the next few weeks, and only if you are continually alert will you ever succeed in housetraining the puppy properly. So if you are out of the house for long periods perhaps some other type of pet may be more suitable.

But – if after due consideration you consider that the only breed for you is a Westie – go on to the next stage, finding a local breeder. You may find this rather difficult, but persevere, it will be worth your while. If you have no luck in tracing a specialist breeder, start at the top. Make enquiries at the Kennel Club for the name and address of the secretaries of the breed clubs. In Great Britain there are three. The West Highland White Terrier Club (of England), the West Highland White Terrier Club (of Ireland) and the West Highland White Terrier Club. Contact the secretaries of these clubs and they will be able to supply you with a list of breeders in your area.

Before making contact with your local breeders, it is important to decide what you want your puppy for, and whether it is to be male or female.

Many people start with a pet Westie and decide they would like to do some showing. So if there is the faintest possibility that you may like the idea, visit a few shows and see what goes on. You may get hooked on showing or you may decide never to enter a dog show again. But at least you are not going to be disillusioned by buying and trying to show a pet quality puppy and getting nowhere with it.

Choosing a puppy for a pet

The most important requirements for a pet are that it should be healthy and of sound temperament. If possible ask to see more than one puppy – sit and watch them for a considerable time.

Try and pick a puppy that fits in with your or your family's temperament. There will be quiet, gentle puppies and boisterous puppies, and these are not necessarily divided according to sex. There can be very gentle loving dogs and tomboys, so that the idea that it is the females who are gentle and loving and the dogs more outgoing and independent is not always true. You may have to choose your puppy before it is ready to leave the breeder, but this will give you time to go home and make all ready for the new arrival. When inspecting the pups ask to see the mother – this should always be possible when you go directly to the breeder. The dam will probably look rather untidy as during the time when she was carrying the litter her coat will have grown. She may be very thin because rearing a litter takes quite a lot out of the bitch and it will be several months before she is back to her former condition. But seeing her will give you some idea of how the puppies may develop and at least you will be able to assess that she has a pleasant temperament. Sometimes you may

Mother Son Grandfather

even be able to see the father, if he is owned by the same person as the bitch, but this is rather unlikely. Before going to collect your puppy when it is about eight weeks old, make its new home ready; a place that it can call its own and a supply of toys to keep it happy.

Things to ask the breeder before you take your puppy home. Most puppies are infested with round-worm when they are born and it is most important that they should have been effectively wormed before they reach eight weeks of age, and you should check that this has been done. Some puppies have rather persistent worms and may need worming more than twice.

Even if your puppy is to be the family pet, it is a good idea for it to be registered with the Kennel Club. This is essential in the case of a bitch, for if she is not registered you will be unable to register any of her puppies, should she have a litter at a later date. You should therefore check that the breeder has this in hand, although it is unlikely that you will be given completed forms at this stage as the registering of puppies with the Kennel Club can take many weeks. However, what the breeder should supply you with is a clearly written pedigree for the puppy, together with a diet sheet and further recommendations for feeding. The other documents that you will receive from the breeder, either then or in due course, are either a partially completed form to enable you to register the puppy with the Kennel Club or a completed Kennel Club registration form with the puppy's official name, plus a form to transfer the puppy into your name with the Kennel Club. This has to be signed by the breeder, so if possible it is easier to collect it at the time of purchase. If you intend to show the puppy it must be transferred into the active register.

Show puppies

It is virtually impossible to say for certain of an eight-week-old puppy that it will be a show winning specimen. All that can be said is that at this time it possesses no outstanding faults that would disqualify it, and that it has the general breed characteristics which, if everything goes as it should, could end up as a puppy than can win in strong competition. There are many things which can go wrong between the ages of eight weeks and six months, which could spoil the puppy for

Left, appealing puppy coat; right, a much better type of coat but not as attractive at this age – eight weeks

the show ring. If you are a novice you will have to rely on the integrity of the breeder, so for a show puppy go to someone who shows the breeds as they can guide you to the best choice.

The anatomy of a show puppy must be sound even at eight weeks. Bent front legs, for instance, will never go straight. On the other hand you can ruin a good front by carrying the dog around incorrectly, and poor feeding will not prove advantageous either.

Read the breed standard and be fully conversant with this. Go to shows and watch Westies being judged. Take a person with you who knows about the breed. These are a few things you can do before going to buy a puppy in the hope of showing it later on. But remember, no one can guarantee its course of development and things can and do go wrong.

General care

In this section I will try to mention a few of the different ways used to raise and house a Westie. Different people have varying methods which they prefer. It is up to you to decide which particular method is best suited to your requirements.

Feeding

The feeding of a small puppy can nowadays be treated in two totally different ways; the devotees of each method swearing by its success.

The first could be called the traditional method of feeding a puppy and is certainly the one quoted by most books on the subject. In this method foods which are normally kept in the kitchen for human consumption are utilised, eggs, meat, milk and cereals being the basis of the diet with calcium and other nutritional elements necessary to the dog being added when required.

The second method has developed over the last few years with the advent of dried foodstuffs, which are now readily available to the pet owner. These foodstuffs come in pelleted or loose form and are a complete food, no meat need be added and they have their full complement of vitamins and minerals. They can be fed dry but in this case a supply of fresh water should always be available, or they can be soaked in water, milk or gravy.

However you decide to feed your puppy, it is most important that it be done well. The animal protein must be given to form substance and muscle, together with bone building foods,

carbohydrates and fats, and the vitamin and mineral supplements already mentioned.

I do not intend to go into the feeding of the prepared dried foods, because, in all cases, it is important when feeding these to follow the manufacturer's advice and instructions carefully.

When you buy your puppy at about eight weeks old, it is important to maintain as closely as possible its feeding routine. So make sure that before you leave the breeder's kennels you have a copy of the diet with times of meals. This will help to avoid an upset tummy which can be brought on by a change of diet.

The following diet is a sound one to work on. Variations may be found to this which can be substituted and as the puppy gets older, say at about ten weeks, it may reject the morning milk feed. This is quite natural as it is growing up. You may find

Mac and Tim

it difficult to decide how much your puppy needs to eat. This can vary from one puppy to another. A good check is to weigh the dog regularly. It will show a gradual but steady weight increase. When cutting out a meal it must be remembered that all the others must be increased in quantity. Meat must be the staple diet and this part of the diet should be increased as the milky part gets less.

Early morning. 8.00 a.m. Warm milk with added cereals, scrambled egg. Milk with baby cereal. (Some puppies cannot digest cows' milk. You may have to substitute a baby milk).

Mid-morning. Small saucer of minced meat, either raw or cooked, together with a small amount of well soaked puppy meal.

Mid-afternoon. Repeat the morning feed – using one of the alternatives.

5.00 p.m. As the mid-morning feed.

Bedtime. Warm milk with the addition of a cereal and honey or glucose.

To one of the milky meals add Stress, Canovel, or a similar preparation according to the instructions on the container.

As this diet is for an eight-week-old puppy it must gradually change. At three months gradually increase all the amounts according to the puppy's growth. By the age of four months a typical diet could be: milk meal with cereals, etc. first thing in the morning, a meat meal at mid-day, with the same in the evening. At the age of seven months the mid-day meal can gradually be decreased until it is eliminated. Do everything gradually and do remember to increase the meals in size as they decrease in number. You should continue to add the Stress or its equivalent until the growing period has finished. At twelve months your Westie should be receiving its adult diet, which will vary according to its size. This should be round about half a pound (quarter of a kilo) of mixed meat and meal.

Table scraps, such as meat fat and vegetables may also be added, and cheese or fish can be used as a useful alternative to meat.

It is unwise to feed a very young puppy on tinned food but by all means use it as an alternative food when the puppy is older. Never give your puppy fish, pork or chicken bones. They can splinter and cause damage to the alimentary canal. If you want to give your puppy a bone ask the butcher to saw, not chop, a piece of marrow bone and give this raw. It gives hours of

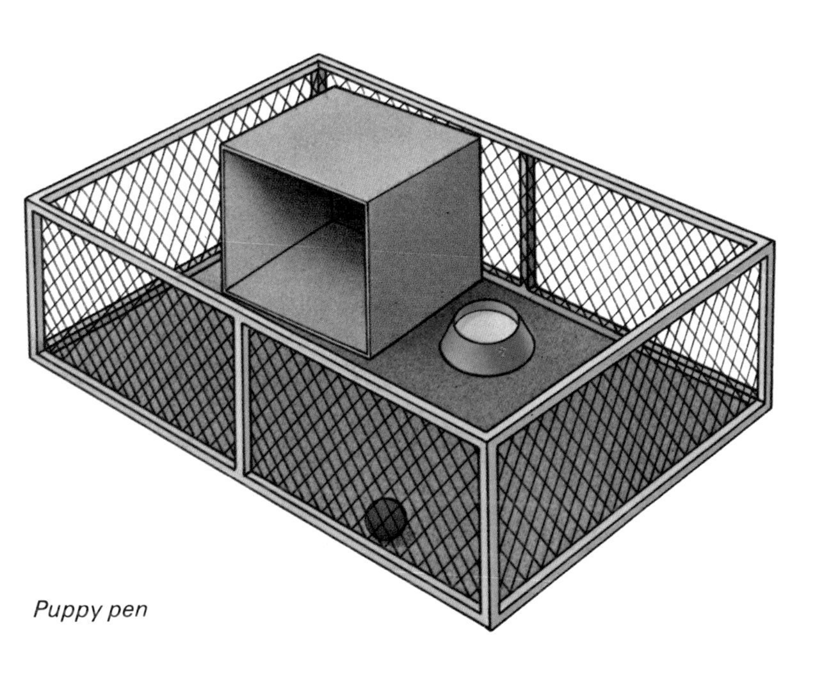

Puppy pen

amusement to the puppy and is good exercise for its teeth. Dog chocs can be given as a reward but avoid the human variety as they are bad for the teeth.

Housing

Again housing a Westie is a matter for personal preference. Being a hardy breed, they can be housed in or out of doors, but whichever you choose the Westie should be provided with a dry, draught-free bed in which to sleep. Its first home in the house can be very simple. In fact perhaps one of the most simple and cheap forms of bed can be a cardboard box with the front cut down. This has several advantages. It can be the correct size for the dog at all periods of growth. A box which is just big enough for it to stretch out in will be much warmer than a large one. The box can be discarded if soiled or chewed. It is free and can be changed every couple of weeks for a size larger. A more permanent bed can be considered when your puppy has finished growing. There are many good types of dog bed on the market, but hygiene should be considered when making a purchase. It may be necessary from time to time to wash the bed and some types can be more thoroughly cleaned than others. There are oval shaped moulded plastic beds in which you can place a dog blanket, or alternatively safari beds. The latter can be covered in a loose cover which can be made to fit in with the decor of the room in which the dog sleeps.

The indoor kennel This type of kennel is usually very convenient if you have more than one dog to house, but should only be used as sleeping quarters. They are not made for housing dogs for long periods of time. This type of kennel is usually constructed of wood. The front is covered with wire mesh and there is a door at the front to admit the dog. Indoor kennels come singly or in mutiples, either stacked one on top of the other or side by side.

The outdoor Westie The first consideration for a well planned outdoor site is that it must be well drained and should be high enough for you to walk into. You should try to place the kennels as near to the house as possible for two reasons. On a wet, wintry day you will find it miserable tramping backwards and forwards to see to the dogs. Also the Westie is a dog that likes human companionship and it will be more likely to get this near the house. If possible visit other kennels and see how their layout works. It is largely a matter of preference how you arrange the buildings and runs.

Try to purchase as large a building as possible so that you have room for expansion. It is advisable to have a construction which allows easy access to all runs and this will necessitate a corridor either along one side or, if it is an extra wide building, down the middle. A compartment of four feet by about six feet (1.20m. by 1.80m.) should be adequate to house two Westies. Outside each compartment can be a run about twelve feet (3.60m.) long. Arranged so that there is a 'pop-hole' in the kennel wall this means that the dog can please itself whether it is in or out. The run can be part concrete, as this is easy to wash down and also good for keeping good feet, and part grass. In the run there should be some shade and a bench. If the latter is about fifteen inches (38cm.) high, the Westie can either lie on top of it or underneath for shade.

The indoor compartment should be provided with a sleeping box for each occupant. As in the indoor kennel, it must be draught free and raised off the ground.

Tiered indoor kennel

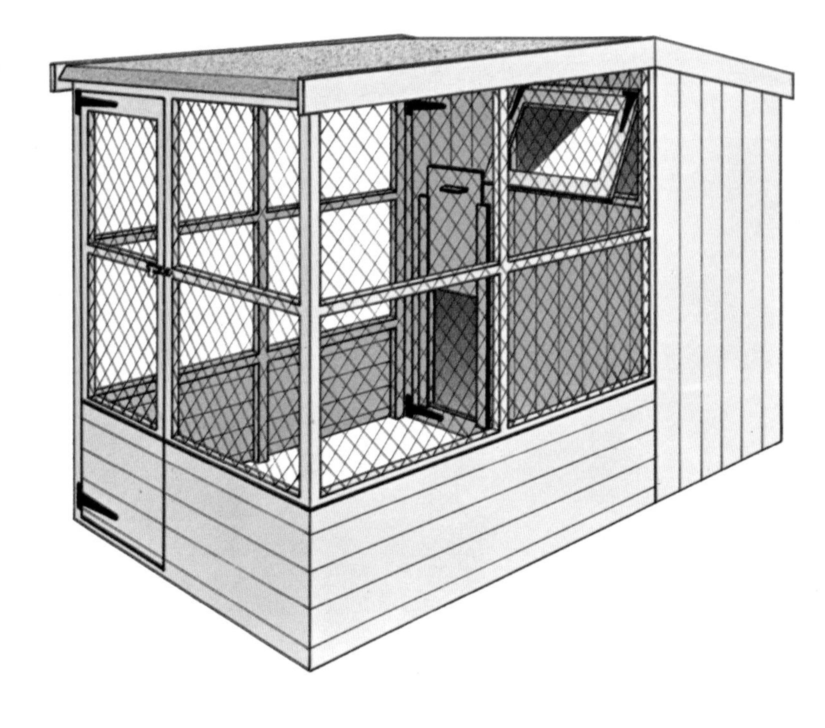

Kennels outdoor

On more general points it is a good idea if there is a door at either end of the building. During a hot summer's day both doors can be open to allow for better ventilation and also it is necessary when thinking of fire precautions to have more than one exit. Another thing that can be provided in a large building is a grooming area with cupboards and a worktop of the right height on which to groom a dog.

In Britain, the Breeding of Dogs Act (1973) makes it necessary to comply with Council regulations, if you have more than two bitches of breeding age. So before starting any structural work it would be a good idea to enquire at the local environment office for more details.

Exercise

A Westie does not demand to be taken on long walks, but a fit one would enjoy a day out without tiring. It is more important that it should receive regular short walks. It is essential that some of the exercise is of a restrained type. By this I mean put your dog on a collar and lead and take it for a road walk. There is nothing that can replace road walking for the development of muscle and nice tight feet. At some time during the day your Westie should be given a free run. Find a place of safety where it cannot run into a road, and also keep it away from farm stock. It is all too easy for a dog to think that sheep are joining in a game of chase. Where there are farm animals keep your dog secure on a lead as it may cause untold harm and you are to blame.

Basic training

Before starting any form of training make sure that the puppy is well settled into its new house and is used to you. It is a much harder job to train a puppy if it is uncertain of its surroundings.

The Westie is an intelligent dog and is therefore quite easy to train. But it is you, the owner, who must learn the first lesson. It is necessary for you to be very patient and to exercise a great deal of self-control. The easiest way to train a puppy is by quietly but firmly repeating the object of the lesson until the dog learns what is required of it. If it fails in its training at any point, you are more likely to be at fault than the puppy.

As soon as the puppy has become adjusted to its new environment and learnt to trust its new owner, training can begin.

The first thing that the new puppy must learn, along with house training, is basic obedience. You must start where you mean to continue. Do not let the dog get away with something as a puppy if you will find it annoying when it is adult. Remember it is the tone of the voice more than what you say that is important. If you reprimand the puppy use a harsh firm tone, and praise should be light and warm. Consistency at all stages in training is essential. If you expect the puppy to learn quickly once you have said 'No' to something, it must not be ignored next time the puppy disobeys.

Housetraining It is impossible to expect a puppy to be totally housetrained before it reaches the age of about five months, for until this time its muscular control is not fully developed.

Paper training can begin as soon as the puppy enters the home. At first spread the paper in all the parts of the house in which the puppy is allowed its freedom. It will soon show a preference for one or two spots, then the rest of the newspaper can be removed. As this habit is established the paper can gradually be moved to the spot you want the puppy to use.

If at all possible the puppy ought to be put outside to relieve itself. If this is done frequently it will soon get the idea of what going out is for. Every time the puppy wakes up it should be put out, likewise when it has eaten or been playing. Stay outside with it and when it relieves itself praise it and take it back inside. If this regular routine is set up, you will no longer require the papers. Do remember that if the routine is broken by you forgetting, it is your fault if the puppy fails.

Lead training As the puppy will be unable to go out of your house and garden until it has finished its course of injections to protect it from hardpad and distemper, some training can be carried out prior to this in the garden.

Place a small lightweight collar on the puppy and allow it to wear this around the garden, but remove it at bedtime. It will soon accept the collar without going crazy everytime it is put on. Next attach a piece of string to the collar and let the puppy drag this around. This can very soon be replaced by a lead. When the puppy no longer bothers about it, pick up the end of the lead and let it take you for a walk around the garden. After this stage you must start to get it to walk in the direction you want to go. Talk to the puppy in a friendly manner and at the same time offer it a small amount of its favourite food. It will

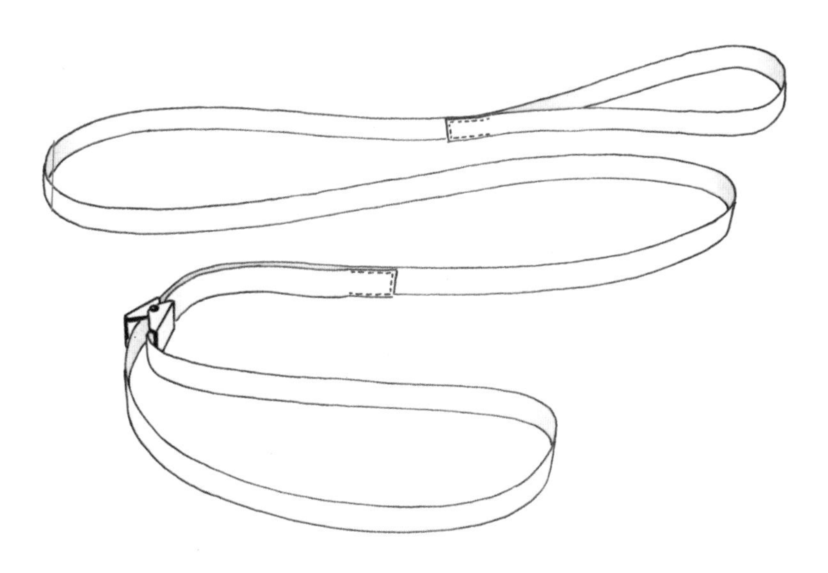

Slip lead

Choke chain

soon learn to follow without the use of bribery.

After basic training, if the dog has started to pull hard on the lead, try using a choke-chain. Never use a harness. This does not stop the dog pulling and will only make it pull out at the elbow. Before using a choke-chain on the dog, make sure that you know how to use it correctly. Assuming that your Westie is to walk on your left hand side, which is the correct side, the chain should pass over the neck onto the side nearest you, and through the ring. When the chain is linked to the lead the weight of the chain hanging under the chin should keep it loose round the neck. Only when the dog starts to resist should you jerk on the collar, releasing the pressure immediately. I would not recommend the use of a choke collar without first seeking the help of someone who knows how to use it. Perhaps the local pet shop might show you how to put it on and use it correctly.

Right from wrong

When a puppy is teething it likes to chew on things. Make sure that you provide things that it is allowed to chew. A puppy should not be expected to know the difference between your new shoes and the old pair it was given. Better to give it something totally different, a marrow bone or a large rawhide chew now available from most pet shops.

Something that the dog should be discouraged from doing at an early age is jumping up at people. As it jumps put your foot up in front of it, at the same time issue the command 'Down!' very firmly.

A puppy must not be allowed to bark simply because you leave it alone. It will surely anger the neighbours. Make the puppy think you are going out. Leave the house but wait, just out of sight, until the puppy starts to bark. The moment it starts shout, 'No! Quiet!' It will soon get the idea.

Never stop your dog from barking at someone coming to the house. When it has warned you of the visitor's approach and you require it to stop, then call 'Quiet!' If the dog persists, hold its mouth closed and repeat the command. A good house dog is a valuable asset.

Grooming

To groom a Westie to perfection is a great skill which may take many years to learn. The majority of people never achieve their aim for it takes many skills grouped together to present the perfectly presented Westie which is the eye-catcher in the show ring. In the hot competition of the championship show, the presentation of your dog can make the difference of several places when all dogs are so good that the judge has to split hairs to divide them. Even the pet Westie can be greatly enhanced by a well-groomed and styled jacket. This is something that every owner can learn to do, even if only to keep the family pet tidy between more thorough groomings by a professional.

The most important thing to remember, when you first think about having your Westie's coat removed by a professional, is that on no account should the coat be clipped. This entirely ruins the texture of the coat and does not correctly remove the dead hair by the roots. If you feel that you are unable to strip your own Westie, find someone who will hand-strip the coat in the correct manner.

I am well aware that to some people it may seem unnecessary to tell a dog owner how to groom his pet. But many novices do not have the faintest idea where to start and it is for them that the next section is written. But before missing out the next few pages, just say to yourself, 'Can I comb through my dog's coat as easily as through my own hair?' If not – read on!

General grooming of your pet

You must always remember that a Westie has two coats, the hard, wiry, straight outer coat which is weather resistant, and the soft inner coat resembling fur. It is this under coat which if not groomed thoroughly and regularly will make it necessary to clip your Westie like a sheep, and ruin its looks for many, many months. It is therefore important to groom both coats thoroughly, at least once a week.

Stand your dog on a table covered with a towel, blanket or carpet to stop him slipping about and becoming frightened. For the thorough weekly grooming use a strong steel comb. Start at the feet and work up to the head, as by this method you are less likely to miss any of the coat. Very gently but firmly

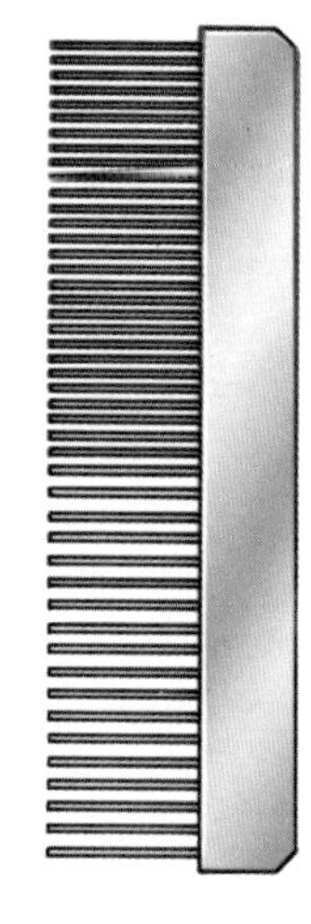

Heavy-backed comb

Metal-handled coarse tooth comb

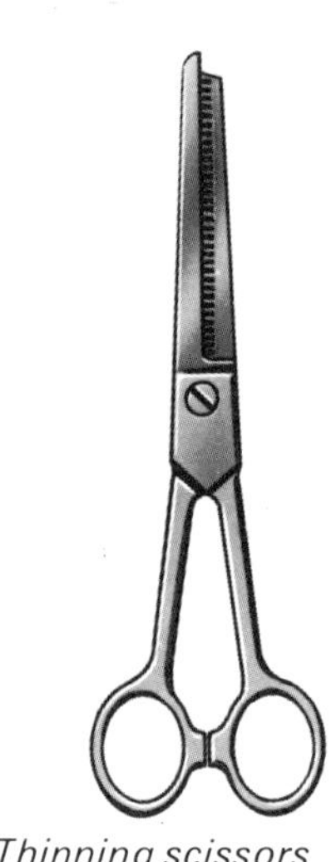

Thinning scissors

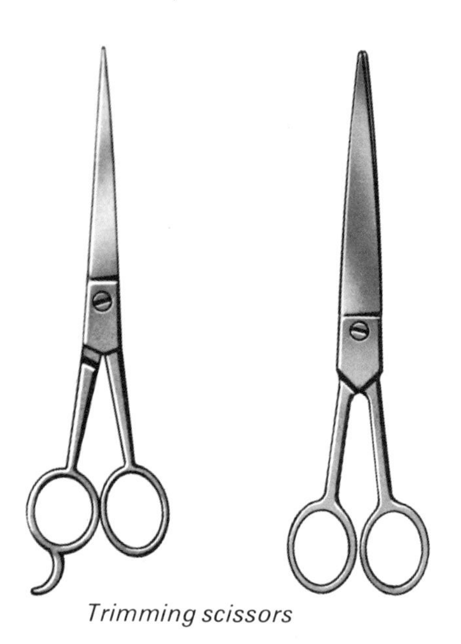

Trimming scissors

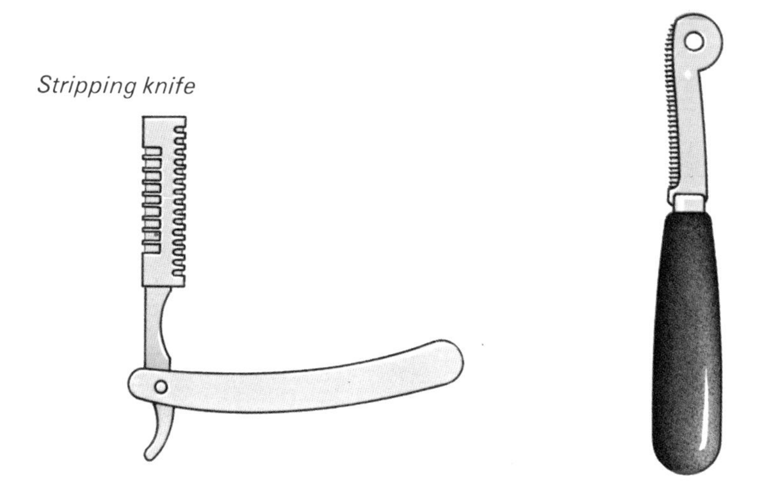

Stripping knife

Magnet stripping knife

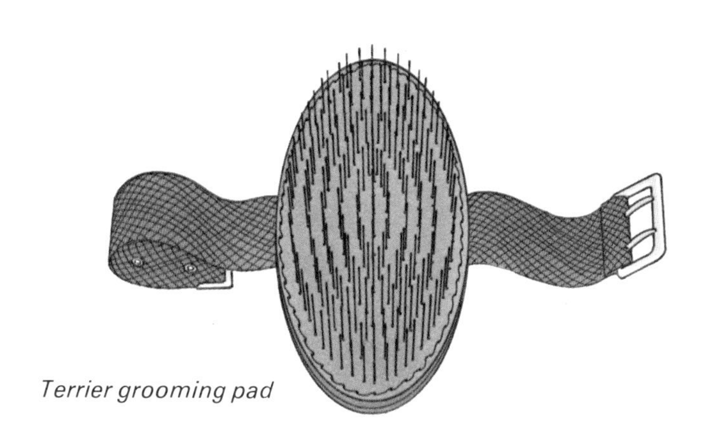

Terrier grooming pad

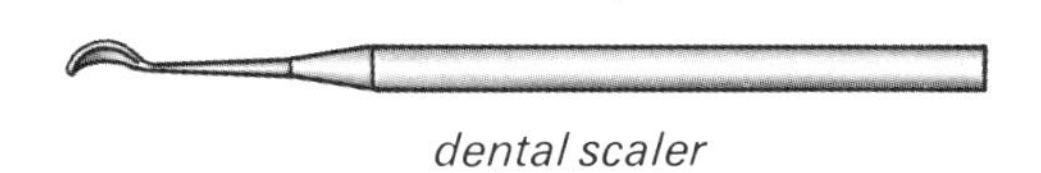

dental scaler

comb through the hair of the legs, paying particular attention to the parts that do not show. Work from the feet, combing right through to the skin and clearing all knots as you work up. Lift the hair above that which you are combing, out of the way. As you finish the first section of hair, let down some more of the hair from above and comb through this. Repeat this until you have completed all the legs. You are most likely to find knots under the arm pits and on the inside of the hind legs. Be very firm about grooming your dog here as many dogs do not like it, but you must insist on finishing the job.

After the legs comb the stomach. If you have a male brush him down underneath and remove any long hairs which have become tangled with a pair of ordinary scissors. Avoid using these if it is possible to tease out the knots. Work through the hair on the underparts in exactly the same way as for the legs, making sure that every piece of hair is knot free. This is the most difficult part of the grooming completed.

Groom the body in exactly the same way as the legs. It is here you will find that, at certain times of the year, large amounts of the furry undercoat will come out in the comb. At these times it is more vital than ever to groom regularly, for it is this coat which, left in for some time, forms a solid felt-like mat. It is because of this that I say, for a thorough grooming, use a steel comb. Brushes, however well used, tend to go through the top coat and straighten that, but do nothing for the undercoat.

Now we are on the last areas, the head and tail. Take the tail first. Comb through the hair at the base, making sure that you comb right down to the skin. Many Westies have a roll of loose skin around the tail and this seems to trap the knots. In the case of the tail groom up to the point. Now do the head. I find it best to comb under the chin first and then around the mouth. The head of a well-groomed Westie should resemble a chrysanthemum with hair growing out from the skin at right angles. Elsewhere the coat should be flat against the body.

You may wonder why I have not mentioned bathing the Westie. This is because it is better to avoid it if possible. The more a Westie is bathed, the dirtier it gets. Bathing tends to remove the natural oils and dry the coat so that it is more likely to tangle. Also, brushing produces static electricity and this in turn attracts the dirt. However, occasional baths may be necessary if the dog has external parasites such as fleas, ticks

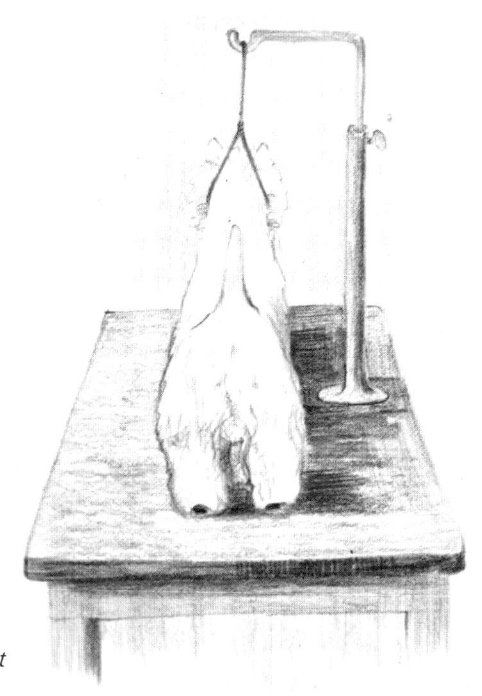

Grooming table and support

and harvest mites, or if the dog rolls in a cow-pat or horse manure. But avoid it unless absolutely essential.

Instead of shampoo, use a dry grooming powder, or a chalk block, or calcium carbonate from the chemist. This should be rubbed thoroughly into the coat and then brushed out again. This is best done in the open air as the chalk will tend to fly everywhere.

When you think you have mastered the grooming correctly, why not have a go at the next stage? It is quite easy really.

Tidying the coat It is now that the basic technique of pulling the outer coat from the dog must be learnt. But why pluck when many people have their Westie clipped? This is entirely wrong. In hot weather the dog is protected by the coat. If it is all removed, there is a risk that your Westie may suffer from sunstroke. If the coat is cut, the roots of the old coat are left in the skin and clog it. Consequently the new growth of hair tends to be soft and fluffy.

The first thing to note is that the hair is always plucked in the direction in which it grows. The action of pulling the hair out,

Stripping the coat

which does not distress the dog if it is done properly as this coat is dead, can be likened to gripping a piece of toilet paper of the folded variety between the thumb and forefinger and quickly removing it from the packet. Using the right or left hand, whichever you find easier, hold the palm downwards with the hand in a relaxed position. Grip a few hairs *very* firmly in the thumb and forefinger and jerk the hand firmly downwards. This is the basic movement used in stripping. To begin with you may find that only a few hairs come out of the dog but this will increase as you gain confidence. To help you grip the hair more firmly, rub a little calcium carbonate onto the coat and put some on your fingers.

The second thing is to put the hand that is not being used for stripping onto the dog next to the coat being stripped. This helps to stop the skin being pulled, or, on a loose skinned dog, following the direction of the pull. These movements are probably the hardest part of stripping to be learnt. The rest is purely artistic depending on how good an eye you have for shape and form. From the point of view of keeping your Westie tidy, this is a relatively unimportant aspect. If, however, you intend showing your dog, it is of paramount importance.

Before commencing to tidy the long hair of the Westie, make sure that it is well groomed. Commence work on the back and neck. The hair on the neck and shoulders should be stripped shorter than the rest of the body. Start at the top of the neck and, taking a few of the longer hairs in the thumb and forefinger, jerk the hair down firmly in the direction of growth. Continue this process down the back and sides of the neck and onto the shoulders, stopping when you are level with the elbows.

Unfortunately with most dogs it is not possible to adopt the same procedure of stripping down the front of the neck, as this part is more tender. For the pet, I would recommend the use of hairdresser's thinning scissors. Used regularly these will keep the hair in front of the chest relatively tidy. Do not use these in a horizontal direction across the dog's chest as you will find that you produce unsightly scissor marks. Instead, place the scissors in the vertical position and cut in the same way that the hair grows. (Do not use ordinary straight scissors for this job).

Follow on to the second section of the drawing. The hair on the neck and shoulders should be the same length as the top of the back. Strip the hair out here until it is relatively short. Continue stripping down the rib cage of the dog, gradually leaving the hair longer as you work downwards. Enough hair should be stripped out of the sides of the coat in order that your Westie should look flat sided.

Now go on to section three. On this part of the Westie most of the hair is left longer, but the shorter hair of the back and sides in the previous section should be blended in. Using scissors again trim the tail to look like a carrot by removing all the hair from behind and on top of the tail, and shortening the hair at the base of the tail. This avoids constant soiling of the rear end and is more hygienic.

I have left the most difficult part of tidying up your pet to the end. It is the most difficult but the most important because, if mistakes are made, it can spoil the good looks of your Westie. The parts to which I refer are the furnishings – head and legs. Let us take the legs first, starting with the front. First comb through the hair thoroughly getting rid of any knots, especially under the arms. Next lift each paw in turn and trim away any long hair from between the pads. Now we are ready to deal

Before and after trimming

Before and after trimming

with shaping the rest of the leg. Using a stripping knife or scissors, look at the dog from the front and trim away any very long hair to make the legs look straight and parallel. Carefully trim around the feet. They should look round and full.

Now look at the dog from the side. Trim a little of the hair from the side of the elbow and behind the legs to make them look straight and sturdy. Now do the hind legs. Tidy up the pads in the same way as the front feet and neaten the long hair on the legs. Remember that leg hair grows very slowly so remove only a little at a time.

Finally we come to the Westie's crowning glory, the head. Start with the ears. Hand strip the top third of the ears. This makes them look small and neat. Now brush the head hair thoroughly. The aim here is to make the head chrysanthemum shaped. Bearing this in mind, using a stripping knife or thinning scissors, take a small amount of hair off at a time, constantly changing view points so that the head does not appear saucer shaped through too much stripping from any one point.

Unless you have a very good eye for shape, your first attempts at stripping may not be too grand but do persevere. A smart, well-groomed Westie is a joy to see and never fails to gain comment when out for a walk.

Care of the teeth Teeth should be examined regularly. Dogs that are allowed to gnaw marrow bones and rawhide chews generally keep their teeth in good condition. Sometimes tartar gathers around the canine and premolar teeth and this must be removed as, if left, it will cause tooth decay. Some dogs are very co-operative and will allow you to remove it with dental scalers. Others need veterinary assistance, in the form of an anaesthetic.

Care of feet and nails Examine these regularly to make sure they are kept in good condition. Trim the hair from between the pads and, using a coarse file (woodworking type), hold each claw separately and file it, stopping before you get to the quick. In a light nail this can be seen as a pink area in the middle. It is more difficult to see in the black nail, but as you approach the quick the nail becomes more spongy.

Show preparation

So you have bought a puppy for show, or that pet puppy that you bought sometime ago has turned out rather nice and you

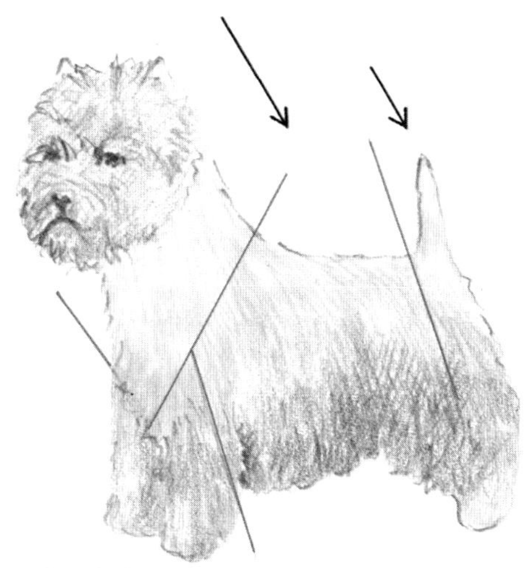

Gradation of coat, from undercoat to full length in the completely trimmed dog

Desired chrysanthemum shape of head

have decided to try your hand at showing. The thing that will most make or mar your success is the presentation of your dog. For show, this can be no easy matter. For some it is a skill relatively easily learnt because they have 'the eye' for it but for others it is a skill they will never acquire. For to strip a Westie and to prepare it to peak show condition are two entirely different things. A pet Westie can be stripped in a couple of hours. The show Westie will take many weeks or months of work, removing sometimes a few hairs at a time, and all the time striving to make your dog look as close to the breed standard as possible.

Show presentation is something that cannot be learnt from a book, therefore I will not go into great detail on this point, for this is a book to help the novice. Once you have assimilated the main points of grooming, and visited a few shows, you will no doubt have found someone who will assist you with the finer points.

The skill is something which must be gained through experience and through watching the experts at work. Visit as many shows as possible and watch people preparing their dogs. Some will be prepared to give you advice, but do wait until after they have finished their preparations before bombarding them with questions. Remember it takes a great deal of concentration to prepare a dog.

The first thing that must happen before you begin the task of show preparation is to accept that no dog is ever perfect. Look at your own dog and recognise its faults, being very honest with yourself. Now try and fool everyone that your dog is perfect by as clever presentation as possible, and by covering up the faults you know exist. But one word of warning – a good judge will never be fooled by presentation. Remember it is his hands that are feeling for perfection as well as his eyes looking for it.

Correcting faults While it is not possible to correct physical faults, it is possible to disguise them by clever presentation. If your Westie has turned out feet, leave hair on the inside of the leg at the bottom and the outside further up. Similarly if the dog roaches its back slightly, leave thicker hair in front of and behind the highest point.

Taping the ears Some puppies have difficulty in getting their ears to stand upright and during the teething period ears can do funny things. Ears that have been erect may even drop.

Camouflage of less desirable faults

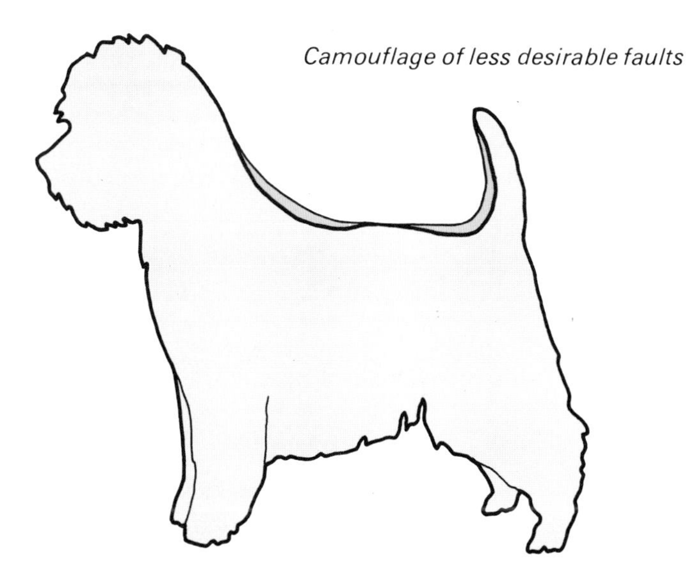

to improve top line and tail set

to improve the front when toes turn in and elbows out

toes turning out

It is important at all times to keep the hair short on the ear fringes. Half an inch of hair on the tips of the ears can be quite enough to hold them down. If it is just the tips of the ears that are uncertain, try painting them with colloidin, both inside and out. This will cause no discomfort and may just stiffen the ear sufficiently.

Some ears do tend to grow rather quickly and may need more than the collodion to get them up. Taping must then be tried. When putting tape onto a puppy's ears never put it on tightly and remove it every few days to check the ears. Always tape both ears together as this makes them work as a pair. Use one piece of tape on each ear. Apply to the back of the ear and bring round to the front, cupping the ear slightly before overlapping the ends of the tape at the front of the ear. Repeat on the other ear even if it is up.

Next, tape both ears together in the correct position. One long piece of tape between the ears will hold them the correct distance apart. Another piece of tape placed at the front of this will cover up the sticky surface and prevent the head hair from adhering to it (see diagrams).

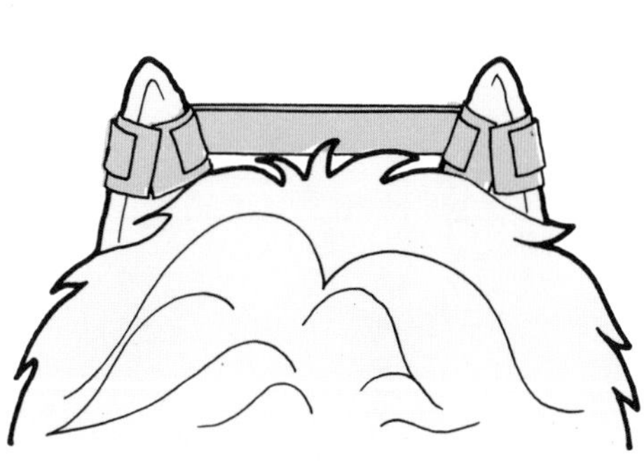

Taping the ears. After each ear has been taped set them the right distance apart and use two long strips of tape to hold them in position. This encourages the ears to work together. Be careful not to trap any of the head hair in this tape.

Exhibiting and show training

If you have bought a puppy in the hope that it may develop well enough to show, it is never too early to start simple training, although nothing must be carried on long enough for the puppy to become bored. Little and often must be the important thing.

After the puppy has completed its innoculations training should commence. In the first stages it will not vary at all from the basic training given to any puppy, in that the pet and the show puppy should feel happy and confident on a lead and should walk close to your left hand side without showing fear or unwillingness.

The main difference between pet and show training at a young age is that the show puppy must get used to many different people handling it without being worried by the attention. Mind you, this is no bad thing for the pet puppy to learn. Nothing can be worse than taking a dog to the vet where, because of fear of the unknown and unfamiliar, the dog will not let the vet or anyone else near it. So put your puppy on a table and gently but firmly groom it. Then gently look at its mouth and teeth while all the time talking quietly to it. When it is used to this treatment from you, ask someone else, who you know will be gentle and firm with the puppy, to look at its teeth and to feel its legs and general construction.

During this period of initial training you should have visited some shows to see how the Westie is shown, for there is a good deal of skill required to get the puppy to show all its merits. At a show you will see how people place their dogs on the table for the judge to examine and how the dog is expected to stand. If possible find out if there are any ringcraft classes in your area and start attending these regularly. Here your puppy will learn to mix with other dogs without getting over excited or frightened, and you will be taught how to get the best out of your puppy. Quite a useful aid to training is a mirror placed on the wall so that, when you have the puppy standing on the table, you will be able to see a judge's view of it, and be able to make sure the pup is standing so as to make the best of itself.

By the time your puppy is six months old, it should stand with confidence on the table with its head held proudly and its tail erect. Allow a complete stranger to look at the teeth and feel all over the dog. After which, when asked to move, the dog should walk along jauntily by your side without a care in the world. Then when back in the line with other dogs, you should be able to stand yours so that it looks its best, making sure that it is standing alert and looking ahead. Check that the feet are in the correct place and that the dog is not standing with its elbows turned out or its back roached, or that you are not pushing the tail too far over the back.

In Britain there are various types of show from Exemption shows run for charity, through Sanction, Limited and Open shows, to the biggest of all, Championship shows. At the latter, the very valued Challenge Certificates are on offer to some or all breeds. These are awarded to the best dog and the best bitch of the breed in question. To become a British champion a dog must win three of these under different judges at different shows.

In America, show categories run from Matches to Speciality and Points shows, the latter being where one can win points towards a championship status for one's dog. To become an American champion a dog must win a total of fifteen points and two of these wins must be 'majors' (three or more points won at the same show) won under different judges. The number of points awarded at a show depends on the number of dogs and bitches of the breed actually present and can also vary from area to area.

The definitions of classes at shows are totally different in Britain and America. All would-be exhibitors should obtain the show regulations from their respective Kennel Clubs and study them. However, in neither country can any dog be shown which is not Kennel Club registered. This is one of the reasons why it is so important to make sure that your puppy is registed when you buy it. It could be very disappointing to get the urge to show or breed and find that one's dog, though pure bred, was ineligible.

Show preparation
The first thing to be done of course is to find out where the shows are and make your entries. The only way to find the shows is to take a copy of one of the dog papers every week. In Britain *Our Dogs* and *Dog World* carry advertisements of the shows with names and addresses of secretaries, where to obtain schedules and the closing date for entries. In America the monthly magazine *Pure Bred Dogs* gives the same type of information.

When you receive the entry forms decide on which classes to enter and fill in all parts of the form accurately and very clearly. It is very easy to make mistakes and not easy for secretaries to decipher some writing. You will have all the details required for entry on your puppy's registration form.

Of course, it goes without saying that the coat of a show dog should receive continual attention to keep it in good condition. Also the inner requirements of the dog should be catered for. A show dog should be in good hard condition with plenty of muscles and not too much fat. The night before the show comes the final preparations. Make sure that your dog is perfectly clean and if necessary wash the muzzle and undercarriage. Then make him as white as possible, doing any extra little bits of stripping that may be found necessary.

Travelling crate

Now get ready all your tools and equipment. A useful addition to the equipment is a small table on which to groom your dog at the show. These are hardly ever provided and it is virtually impossible to groom the dog on the floor. Remember to take the exhibitor's passes if these have been sent out to you before the show.

Aim to arrive early. If it is a championship or points show you should aim to arrive at least an hour, if not more, before judging is scheduled to begin. There is usually such a lot to be done and arriving early will give you a little time to relax before going into the show ring.

Big shows are usually benched and the number on your pass corresponds to the bench number. So the first thing to do when you arrive is to find the bench and install your charge comfortably and safely on it. With the Westie this can be in one of two ways. The first, the traditional way, is with a well fitting collar and a bench chain. The bench chain is not like a lead for it has two clips, one at each end and several swivel joints. The other method of benching is in a box or crate with the top and front made of wire. They are extremely good because the dog feels safe in a box with which it is familiar. These boxes can

The show bench

also be used for transporting the dog to the show and at other unbenched shows.

When your dog is settled, give yourself and your dog a drink and complete the final grooming, making sure your dog is absolutely clean. Nothing looks worse in the ring than a 'grey' Westie.

Make sure that when your class is ready to go into the ring, you do not keep the judge or stewards waiting. If you are unfamiliar with dog shows and are not in the first class, watch to see what is expected of you and your dog. From the time you enter the ring try to be calm because it is amazing how your mood and manner will transmit themselves to the dog.

Whatever procedure the judge chooses to adopt it is up to you to follow. Normally, after you have entered the ring and received your number, a check is made to make sure everyone is present. Then dogs and handlers will be asked to move around the ring. The dog is usually led in the left hand so, in order that the judge sees the dog and not your legs, you must move anti-clockwise around the ring.

Correct show stance

After the judge is satisfied that he has seen all the dogs, he will ask you to stop and then each handler shows his dog as an individual. Put your dog on the table and smooth the coat into place. Pose the dog to show off all its good points. No conversation should take place between you and the judge, but he is likely to ask you its age. Answer clearly and do not elaborate at all.

When the judge has finished he will ask you to move your dog. Some judges like to see the dog move in a triangle in order to see movement from the side, others only want the dog to move away and back again.

Make sure you do what the judge wants. Try to move your dog at a fairly brisk pace and on a loose lead. If the dog is 'strung up' tightly, it will not move naturally.

When the judge has seen you, move back to your place or to where the steward directs you and let your dog relax until the judge has finished looking at the rest of the class. Again pose your dog as well as you can and keep your attention on the dog. If you are picked out for an award move to the place indicated but do not relax until the judge has marked his book because until he has done this, the judge can always change the placings.

As soon as your dog has finished in the show ring return it to its bench. Go back to the ring yourself and watch. You can learn a lot from the more experienced exhibitors.

One thing that must be said about showing, is that it is for the enthusiast only. Can you imagine setting off to a show in the early hours of the morning – travelling hundreds of miles – showing in possibly one class and arriving home late at night? A great deal of pleasure can be gained from producing a dog to perfection and many happy hours can be spent at shows. You will make friends from all over the world and from all walks of life in the pursuit of dog showing. When you only get pleasure from winning a first prize and go home miserable and disgruntled because you have won nothing, then is the time to stop showing, and to choose another hobby.

"Once round, please"

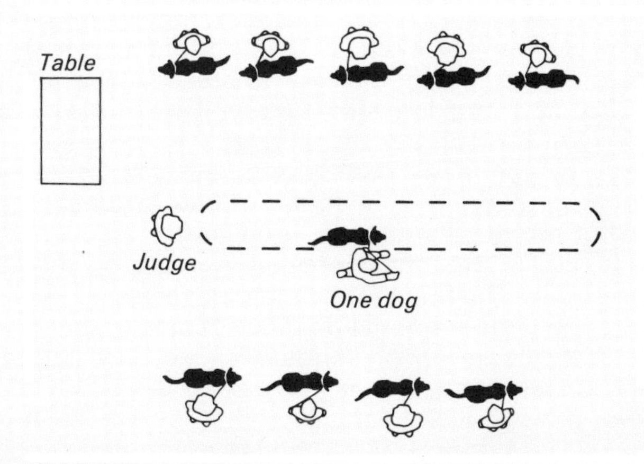

"Once up and down, please"

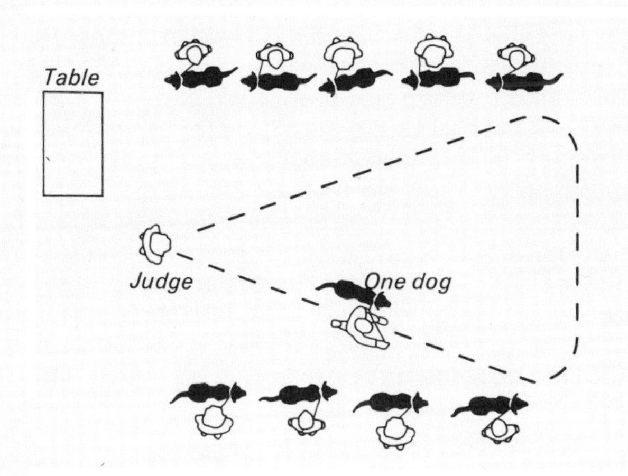

"Triangle, please"

Breeding

If you have decided before buying a Westie that you are eventually either going to use it at stud, if it is a dog, or have some litters, if it is a bitch, it is important to get the best specimen that you can obtain. For to breed from a bitch with faults, or to use a stud dog with faults, will nearly always end in some or all of the puppies developing the same fault, which may carry on for many generations and can be extremely disappointing. There is an element of luck in breeding good puppies but sound parents are a good start.

A great deal of thought is needed in choosing the correct mate for a bitch. The first thing should be to assess her merits and faults and temperament and those of the prospective stud dog. Do not double up on faults because they will almost certainly appear in the litter. If you wish to develop a strain of your own, always stick to the type that is your ideal of the breed. It is more important to choose a dog which complements your bitch than to go to one of the top show winners which may not necessarily fit in with your line and type.

Inbreeding and line breeding

These can be good for the breed if done carefully with a great deal of thought. Inbreeding is not common in Westies, but is the term applied when mother and son, or father and daughter, or brother and sister, are bred together. It is a way of fixing type but it is absolutely essential that both the dog and bitch should be as near perfect as possible. Temperament should be as sound as possible as any faults will intensify with this type of mating. It is not wise for a novice to attempt this without first seeking advice from an experienced breeder.

Line breeding is to mate less closely related animals such as grandfather to granddaughter or half-brother and sister. Unless both the dog and bitch are both good specimens this is not likely to achieve much.

The stud dog

The stud dog should be strong and masculine, not necessarily ready for a fight but looking like a stallion with a proud head carriage and a well arched neck. Nothing can make a dog look so impressive as when he meets a bitch that has come to be mated.

There is no cut and dried method of handling a stud dog during a mating. Some dogs like to be given assistance and others will refuse entirely to go near the bitch if you are holding her. To the novice, I would say that it is something again where you need to get someone with experience to help you. A dog wrongly handled in the initial stages can be put off stud work for some time.

One thing that is most important is that a pedigree dog and a pedigree bitch should never be left alone to mate themselves. Damage can be done to the dog and it is necessary to be able to inform the owner of the bitch if the mating was successful or not.

A Westie can be first used at stud when he is about ten or eleven months old, but he should not be used very often until he is more mature. A dog used too much when he is young will quite frequently become bored and go off stud work for a while.

It is a good idea, if possible, to use the same place each time you use your dog at stud. This enables the dog to become used to a set routine. Some owners like the dog and bitch on a table

The first sign of the approaching season in a bitch is the swelling of the vulva

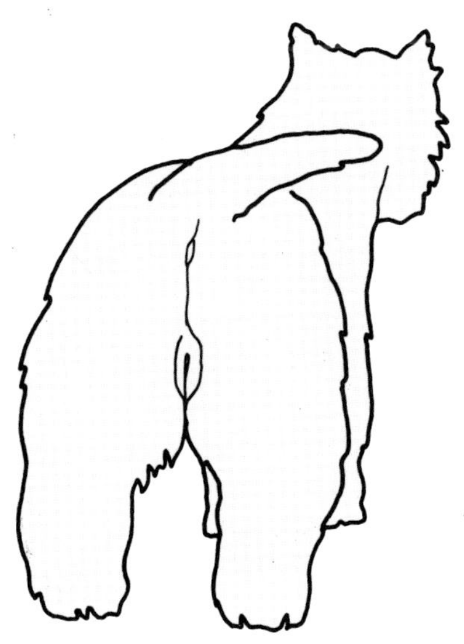

for mating. This certainly has the advantage of being able to mate the dog and bitch in more comfort. If a table is used it is advisable to have an assistant available to steady the bitch.

The bitch

The bitch can come into season for the first time between the ages of six and twelve months of age or even later, but about ten months is average. It is not wise to mate the bitch the first time she is in season because she will be immature and many breeders believe that once the bitch has been mated natural growth stops. So allow your bitch to go through her first season normally.

If you intend to breed from her at a later season, the first 'heat' can be a very valuable time to find out if your bitch has any peculiarities. You will be aware that at a period sometime after six months of age she should be coming into season, so keep a careful eye on her during this time. The first sign of her approaching season is the swelling of the vulva. This can be anything up to about a month before the actual season starts. Try now to check her daily for the red discharge, which is the actual start of her season. When this occurs make a note of the date.

To begin with the discharge will be heavy and dark red but as the days pass the discharge will lessen and will become clearer and paler in colour. At about the twelfth day the discharge will become clear, and it is at this time that she will be ready to accept the dog. It is important that you learn facts like this about your own bitch, because it will be a help to the stud dog owner when arranging the mating. Some bitches are ready for mating before the twelfth day and this is usually evident in the discharge stopping much earlier. Others 'show colour' until much later. It is not unknown for bitches to be mated as late as the twenty first day and to have a litter.

It is usual for a bitch to set up a pattern in the frequency of her seasons. Some have them every four and a half months, others go over the six months. One bitch I know only comes into season once every fourteen months. Remember it is after your bitch has stopped showing colour that she can be mated by a dog, so keep her well away from other dogs until at least the twenty first day of her season.

When you decide to mate your bitch, inform the owner of the chosen stud dog immediately she comes into season. Give as much information as possible about the day you will bring your bitch to be mated. The knowledge gained at her previous season will enable you to do this. The day before you are due to go, confirm your arrangements with the owner of the dog. Make an appointment for your time of arrival so that the dog can be ready to receive your bitch.

The mating

When you take your bitch for mating you may or may not be required to help the stud dog owner by holding your bitch

An emergency muzzle may be used to prevent the bitch from snapping at the stud dog

during the mating. It comes as a great surprise to many bitch owners that their otherwise calm pet can become quite irate when the dog first tries to mount her. However, in the maiden bitch, this is usually because she is nervous and you can help by talking quietly to your bitch and reassuring her. If she is allowed to fidget the dog may be injured.

During the mating of a dog and bitch they usually achieve what is called 'a tie'. At this time it is impossible for the dog to move away from the bitch but he will usually lift one hind leg over the bitch's back so that they are standing tail to tail. They can remain like this for a few minutes or many. The 'tie' is not necessary for a bitch to conceive, in fact some dogs never 'tie' and sire litters without missing. After the bitch has been mated keep her quiet for a few hours.

If the mating has been successful there is little point in repeating it and, if you have used a popular dog, the owner of the stud dog may not be able to fit this in because of other commitments.

It is most important that at the time of mating you receive a copy of the dog's pedigree from his owner. At the same time you should pay the stud fee. Remember it is the mating that you are paying for and not a litter. If the bitch misses, the stud dog owner may give you a free service next time your bitch comes into season, but this is not necessarily so. Check at the time of mating if the owner of the dog is agreeable to this arrangement, and notify him immediately if she does miss. Do not expect to go to him in six months time and claim the repeat mating.

Care of the bitch

After the bitch has been mated take her home and treat her as normally as possible. The gestation period is normally sixty-three days so there is plenty of time to make all the preparations necessary.

During the first five weeks of pregnancy it is very difficult to detect a change in the bitch's physical condition. If you are very observant you may notice that she has become quieter and more affectionate.

Resist the temptation to start giving her more food to eat immediately because this will get her fat and also increase the size of the puppies which will make it more difficult for the bitch when they are born. As the time passes reduce the amount of biscuits she was having and concentrate on giving her good quality food. Feed extra meat either raw or uncooked, and add eggs to her diet. If she was used to having one large meal a day, it may be more comfortable for her if you split this into two smaller meals. Always remember it is the quality of the food more than the quantity which matters most for a bitch in whelp.

By the time the bitch is in her seventh week she will have quietened down considerably. It is generally better to allow the bitch free exercise now although some like to go for a walk, but never over exert her.

If you feel happier take your bitch to the vet and ask him to check her over. At the same time let him have the date on which she is due to whelp so that he can come to your assistance if help is needed.

Whelping

It is quite normal for a bitch to whelp anything up to four days early so have all preparations carried out well in advance. It is a good idea to have had the place where she is going to have the puppies ready for two or three weeks. Encourage the bitch to sleep there during the rest of the time she is in whelp and she will become accustomed to it.

The whelping box itself need not be an expensive piece of equipment. It can very easily be made at home. It should be large enough for the Westie to lie down flat with ample room left for the puppies – about 30in. (75cm.) by 24in. (30cm.) is a good size. Around the insides of the box about 2in (5cm.) up from the base should be fixed a rail. If this is made of dowelling and screwed in from the outside, it can be removed when the puppies are older. The purpose of this bar is to prevent the mother from lying on the puppies and trapping them against the sides of the box. The box should be draught proof and fitted with a lid.

The puppies will require some extra heat during the first few weeks of life and it is a good idea to have an infra-red lamp available. This can be fixed above the whelping box on a chain so that the height can be varied according to the temperature required. This is better and more economical than trying to keep the whole of the room hot enough for the puppies. Even in the hottest of summers puppies will require some extra artificial heat during the night.

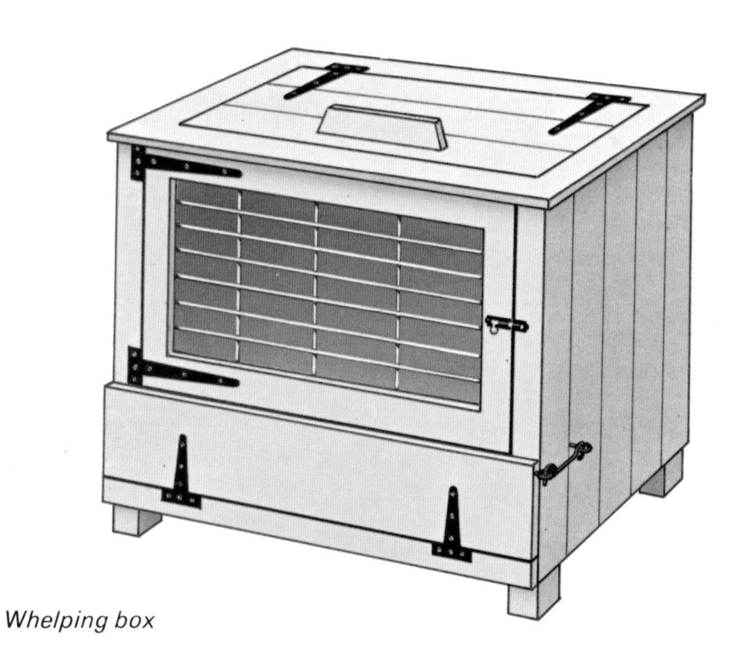

Whelping box

The floor of the whelping box should be covered with a wad of newspapers perhaps up to an inch thick. The only other requirements are cotton wool, clean sheeting ripped up into small pieces about one foot square, towels, an antiseptic, a basin and a pair of sharp scissors.

The first sign that your bitch is about to whelp is usually when she refuses a meal. This may be up to twelve hours before the actual whelping begins. She will probably become very restless and start ripping up the pieces of newspaper in the bottom of the box in order to make herself a nest.

There are some people who think that the bitch should be left to get on with the whelping by herself, but I do not think this is a good idea. Your presence by the side of the bitch may be reassuring for her and you will be there to assist if necessary.

It is quite clear from the bitch's actions when labour has actually begun. She becomes more restless, usually pants very quickly and also trembles. The length of time from the onset of labour to the production of the first puppy varies from bitch to bitch, but keep an eye on her and note carefully when she starts to strain. If she does not produce her first puppy within about an hour of starting to strain, it will be a good idea to consult your vet. He may think it necessary to come round and see how the bitch is progressing.

The first puppy may be preceded by a water bag. This can easily be mistaken for a puppy but is in fact a skin or membrane containing a greenish black fluid. Its size and shape vary according to the length of time it has taken to pass. It may not remain whole, bursting before it comes away from the bitch and releasing the fluid which will drain out of the bitch and be absorbed by the newspaper.

Each puppy is contained in a sack or membrane forming a protection during the birth. If the puppy is partly born and the bitch is having difficulty in pushing it out, this is a time that you can give some help. Using a piece of sheeting, grasp the part of the puppy that is showing and as the bitch strains pull slowly but firmly downward and through the bitch's hind legs.

Puppies normally arrive head first but occasionally arrive hind legs first. This is called a breech birth and can be the cause of difficulty. It is important to get the puppy away as quickly as possible. Ease out the hind legs and the hips and gently but firmly hold the whelp round its waist and pull in a downward direction through the bitch's legs. Speed is essential because if

Bitch with two-day-old litter of four

the sack is broken the whelp will be unable to breathe and will very quickly die. In this situation there is no time to call a vet, the puppy must be got away rapidly in order that it may live and to allow the further puppies to be born. If the bitch is allowed to strain away for some time getting nowhere she will soon become very tired endangering the lives of further puppies.

If the bag in which the puppy is born has not been broken, break it quickly. The easiest place to do this is under the puppy's chin. Clear the sack and any mucus from around the puppy's head and make sure that it can breathe properly. After you have done this, remove the rest of the bag from the puppy and, after waiting for about a minute or so, cut the umbilical cord with a pair of sharp, sterilised scissors about an inch and a half from the puppy. This will dry up and drop off in a day or two. Dry the puppy as quickly as possible and leave it with the mother. After a short while she will begin to strain again, and in time produce another puppy. There is no knowing how long she will take to produce the litter but if at any time she appears to be straining and getting nowhere, call in the vet.

It is a good idea to have a small box with a hot water bottle and towel in it. This can be used as a place to put the puppies already born while the bitch is having others.

After the bitch has finished whelping let her settle down with the litter and rest. Give her a good drink of milk. For the first twenty four hours after whelping the bitch should only be fed on liquids. After this, if her temperature is normal, she will be ready for more solid foods. Several small meals will be much better for her, along with plenty to drink.

Although many people do not bother, I think it is a good idea

One-day-old whelp

to get your vet to come and check the bitch and puppies when she has finished whelping. He will usually give her a check over to make sure that there are no puppies left and give her an injection to stop infection.

For the first few days after the puppies are born you will probably have to encourage the mother to go outside to relieve herself, as she will be unwilling to leave them alone for long.

It is quite refreshing for the bitch to have her tail and rear end washed, as the discharge, if left, will soon become unpleasant.

Westies usually have their dew claws removed at about five days old, but on no account should their tails be docked. I have heard of several litters where this has happened because the owner of the bitch left the puppies alone while the vet did the claws.

Check the puppies each day to make sure that the mother is keeping them clean, and once a week cut their nails.

After about two weeks the puppies eyes will start to open, and their ears a little later. From now on, with good food and regular attention, your litter of pups will begin to become more active and each one will start to develop its own character.

Rearing the puppies

Weaning to eight weeks

The way in which puppies are reared, weaned and housed is very important to their future development. It is at this stage that the temperament, character and structure are formed and no aspect should be overlooked in getting the environment and conditions as perfect as possible for them.

At about three to four weeks old they will become interested in the food and drink you are giving to the mother and this is the time you must start to wean them. Offer them a saucer of milk. This should be the fortified puppy milk such as Ostermilk or Lactol, ordinary cows' milk not being rich enough. To begin with, their noses will have to be directed towards the milk, and a hand held gently behind them will stop them walking backwards. Sometimes it takes a little patience to get them going but they soon get the idea.

At first two milk meals a day should be provided, as most of the nourishment will still be from the dam. After about a week of milky feeds, they seem to become hungrier and now is the time to give them something more solid. Finely scraped meat should be given at first. Feed each puppy separately so that you can be sure each one is getting a share. Every few days the number and quantity of the meals should be stepped up and by five weeks they should have five meals

Six weeks

Six-week-old puppy with rather soft profuse coat

a day, some of which will be meat and fine meal and others scrambled egg or milk.

At about this time (five weeks) the puppies should all be thoroughly dosed for roundworm and the correct dose should be repeated in two weeks time. This should mean that they are free from worms when you sell them.

By seven weeks old the pups should be thoroughly independent of their mother, each feeding from its own dish.

During the time that the puppies are being weaned, the bitch will become less interested in them and by five weeks she will be away from the pups for quite long periods of the day. After she has been fed she must not be allowed to return to them for several hours as there is a possiblity that she will regurgitate her food for them. If this consists of quite large pieces there is a danger that the puppies may choke on them. An alternative to this is to feed the bitch minced food.

When mixed feeding begins the bitch will stop cleaning up after her puppies and this is the time to start encouraging clean habits. Place a large sheet of newspaper outside the puppy box and give the puppies free access to this at all times. This avoids them soiling their bed and starts in an elementary way to paper train them.

At eight weeks old it is time for the puppies to start going to their new homes. Decide which, if any, you are going to keep. When a puppy goes to its new home, make sure that you give to the new owners, at the time of its departure, a diet sheet showing precisely what it has been used to eating, a clearly written pedigree form and any Kennel Club papers that you have for it.

Health

A healthy dog is active, clear eyed, alert and interested in everything that goes on. Changes in the animal's usual behaviour should always be investigated in case they herald some health problem. An energetic dog which becomes lethargic, a greedy dog which refuses food, a dog which scratches continually or rubs part of its body on the floor, a dog which has a discharge from eyes, ears, nose or vagina, all these are displaying symptoms that something is wrong and you should not rest until you have found the cause and had it treated.

One of the most reliable guides to the seriousness of the situation is to take the dog's temperature. Normally this is 101.5°F (38.5°C) and is taken in the rectum. Stand the dog on a table and insert the bulb end of a well greased thermometer about half an inch into the anus. Most dogs do not object but if you are apprehensive, get someone to hold the dog for you thus preventing the possibility of any accident. A temperature of 102.5°F (39.2°C) or over means that a vet should be consulted without delay.

If you are having to give medicine to a dog, do not administer it by putting it on the dog's meal. A sick dog will often refuse food, or eat very little, and then you have no means of knowing how much of the dose has been taken. Pills can be disguised in titbits such as cheese or small cubes of cooked liver. Give an undoctored piece first to allay suspicion. Pills can also be poked down a dog. Get the animal in a position where it cannot back away and open its mouth. Place the pill as far down the back of the throat as possible, close the dog's mouth and hold its head up until it has swallowed. After giving a pill you should always watch carefully for a minute or two as some dogs are very cunning about spitting out pills unobserved some time after you feel sure they have been safely swallowed.

Powdered drugs can be given by sprinkling on the tongue. It is easier to give liquids from a small bottle than a spoon. Make the dog sit and hold its head up with the mouth closed. Pull out a small pouch of skin at the corner of the lower lip and pour the liquid down, keeping the head raised until the dog has swallowed.

Ears that are dirty, smelly or discharging need veterinary

In order to give liquid medicine

To give a pill

attention as untreated ear conditions can become chronic. Never poke anything down a dog's ears. The only part that is safe for an amateur to clean is the inside ear flap which can be wiped over with a dilute antiseptic solution, taking care that no liquid goes down the ear canal itself.

Discharging eyes can be caused by dust, grit or draughts, or can be a symptom of a number of more serious illnesses in which case the dog will usually also have a rise in temperature.

A dog which has plenty to chew rarely has dirty teeth. However the mouth should be examined fairly regularly in case tartar, which looks like a brown crust, is developing on the teeth. In mild cases this can be rubbed off but it may need professional scaling.

All dogs have two anal glands situated just inside the anus. These are normally emptied when the bowels are evacuated. However if the dog has a diet which produces rather soft faeces, the discharge in the glands may build up causing the dog discomfort. The animal will rub its bottom on the ground and will smell badly. It is not difficult to empty the anal glands by manipulation but it is better to watch a vet do it before attempting it oneself.

Dogs vomit very easily so a single bout of sickness is no cause for undue alarm. Continual vomiting, with or without a rise in temperature, needs quick professional diagnosis as a number of conditions giving rise to this symptom are serious.

Mild attacks of diarrhoea are fairly common in the dog which is a natural scavenger. They can also be caused by a change of diet or a mild chill. Treatment in the adult dog is to keep it warm and resting and withhold all food and water for twenty four hours. For the next two or three days, allow the dog water (not milk) and a diet of boned fish or white meat with rice. If the symptoms persist for more than forty eight hours, or if the diarrhoea is violent and accompanied by vomiting, or if there is blood in the faeces, get veterinary advice quickly.

The dog has a number of external parasites including fleas, lice and mites. These cause the dog to scratch and bite at its skin and are usually detected by the owner during a grooming session. The black specks which are the excreta of fleas show up particularly clearly in the white coat of a Westie. Bathing with an insecticidal shampoo is the best way of ridding the dog of these pests.

Roundworms are the commonest internal parasite and can

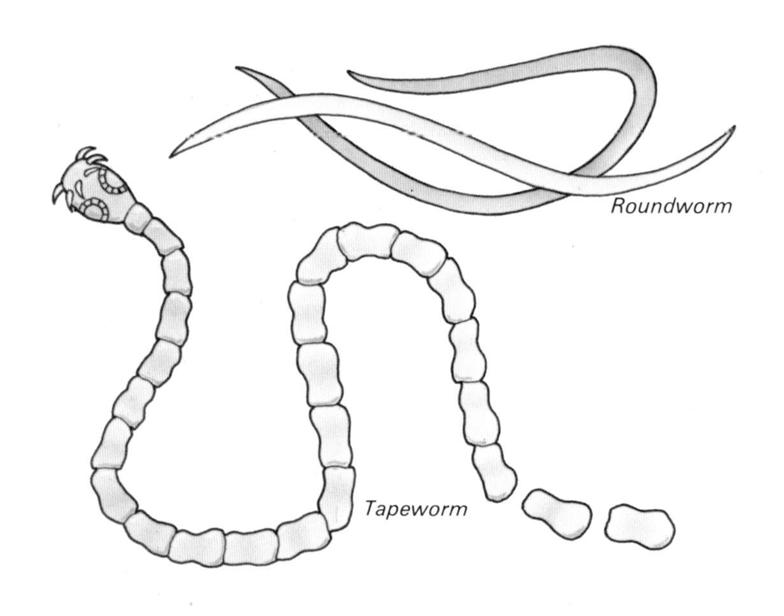

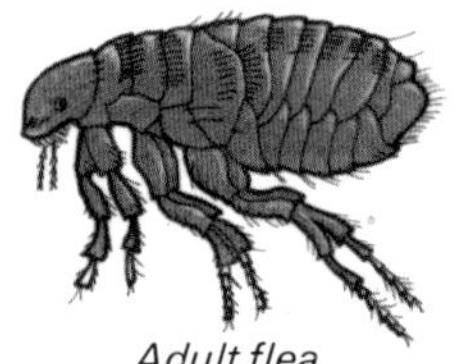

Adult flea

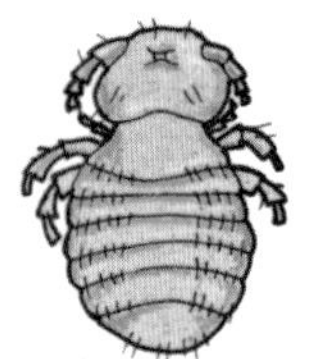

Biting louse

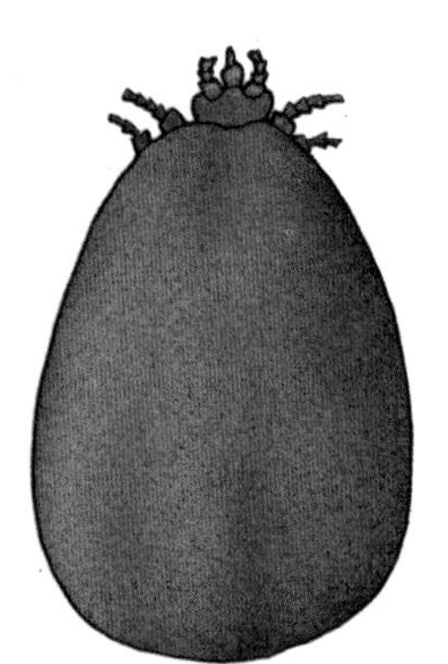

Engorged female tick

Mite (microscopic)

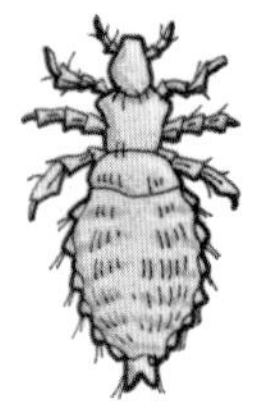

Sucking louse

Parasites

have a serious effect on puppies and their growth. Always make sure that any puppy you buy has been wormed before purchase and get advice from the breeder as to when it should be done again. The presence of worms of any kind in the adult dog is rarely detectable until the worms are either coughed up or appear in the faeces. For accurate diagnosis as to which type of worm your dog has, take a faeces sample to your vet, who will then prescribe the appropriate drugs.

All puppies should be inoculated against distemper, hardpad and the two types of leptospirosis. A combined vaccine confers immunity but needs an annual booster injection. All these diseases are very serious, if not fatal, and *every* puppy needs inoculation before being allowed to meet other dogs or frequent areas where other dogs have been.

I am indebted to my vet for information and help given to me in writing the following. I wish to avoid stressing too strongly any disease or illness, but the three conditions listed below are known to occur in the breed.

The greatest cause for visits to the vet by Westie owners (approximately nine out of ten cases) is undoubtedly skin trouble. Some Westies do seem to be prone to this, while some lines are completely free. The skin allergy can be of two different types. The first type usually occurs on the upper surface of the body or all over and causes general itchiness. If it occurs at certain times of the year the irritation can be caused by pollen or even bright sun. The latter can occur if the dog has very little coat to protect its back. The skin becomes red and the coat becomes brown because the dog continually bites its back making the irritation worse. If the Westie is itchy all over the body it is most likely to be an allergy to its food or some part of it. It will need careful regulation of the food over many weeks to find out exactly what disagrees with the dog. Some Westies become itchy if given certain types of meal, others occasionally benefit by abstaining from red meat.

The second type of allergy is that of contact. It may be caused by nylon carpets, in which case either the nylon carpet has to go or the dog has to be kept off it. It may be caused by newsprint or any of many different things. In a contact allergy it is more normal for the underside of the body to be affected. Here again the condition is exacerbated by the dog continually licking and biting the affected parts.

As the Westie is susceptible to skin disorders, any small

Sit!

lesion should be treated without delay before it becomes a major problem.

Allergies can manifest themselves at any age and with patience can usually be contained, controlled or cured. The following conditions crop up at precise times and for the owner of a young pup become very distressing, but it is better to be aware of the things that can go wrong with your puppy.

If you buy a puppy you are unlikely to come across the first complaint which is a problem for the breeder. This is known as 'Dry Eye'. The name is given because of the symptoms which cause it. The eyes are dry and consequently become very sore and inflamed due to the lack of natural moisture present in the eye. The cause of this disorder is the total lack of a tear duct.

The next complaint has a very long name, craniamandibular osteopathy, known in short as C.M.O. It occurs in puppies between three and five months of age. The symptoms are a thickening of the bone in the region of the back teeth. It can be detected by a swelling under the lower jaw. It is very painful, the puppy refuses to be touched and finds difficulty in eating. However, at this time the puppy is also cutting its second teeth so do not jump to the conclusion that these symptoms are C.M.O. They are far more likely to be its teeth hurting the puppy. This complaint can be treated by a vet but affected puppies should not be bred from.

Probably the most alarming complaint which a Westie can suffer, in common with other short legged terriers indigenous to Scotland, is Perthes disease. This is known by many different names, pseudo leg Perthes and Perthes being two. It is a disease found in young children as well as in dogs. In some ways dogs are a lot better off because they have another three legs to use. The condition is extremely painful and the dog will walk around on three legs holding one hind leg in the air. It can occur at anytime between four and ten months of age. The

result of the disease is that the head of the femur completely disintegrates.

There are many theories as to the cause and many claims made about where it comes from, but as yet there is no real proof known to the veterinary profession. Until that time comes and until more serious research is done into the disease, any animal that has suffered from it should certainly not be used for breeding. Puppies affected by Perthes disease can be given pain killing injections to help them over the worst stage, or they can have a surgical operation to remove the head of the femural bone. If this is done the muscles of the leg take over from the bone and within a few weeks the puppy can be walking about happily on all four legs.

Fortunately C.M.O. and Perthes are not too common but because they do occur in the Westie it is sensible to know of their existence.

Like everything in life, nothing is ever perfect. Let us hope that in the near future these health problems of the Westie may be a thing of the past due to open and serious discussion between breeders and the veterinary profession and researchers in Universities.

The breed worldwide

Today the Westie is very popular in many countries of the world. Dogs have been exported from Britain to start, improve and strengthen the breed world-wide.

America in particular has imported many dogs from the British Isles and many of the top kennels are founded on British bloodlines. The first in the breed to become an American Champion was a British bred dog, Clonmel Cream of the Skies. One of the earliest dogs to join the ranks of champions in America was Ch. Ray of Rushmoor. This dog was later joined by several 'Wolvey' champions, and these in turn were followed by famous dogs from the Hookwood and Branston Kennels.

One of the first to introduce the breed into Canada must have been Mr. Victor Blochin. In 1927 he went to Canada from Scotland taking with him a Westie dog. Mr. Blochin is the owner of the Bencrachan prefix.

In 1951 the West Highland White Terrier Club of Canada was formed. They hold a Speciality Show each year. The most important All-breed Shows are held in Toronto, Ottawa, British Columbia, Montreal and Quebec. As Canada is such a large country exhibits from opposite sides of the country very rarely meet in compeition.

The West Highland White Terrier Club of Australia was formed in 1963 and its first show was held in 1964. The honour of going Best in Show at this event went to English Ch. Busybody of Branston.

Now that dogs can be flown to Australia and New Zealand many more dogs are likely to join their English relatives out there.

The breed is very strongly represented in many countries in Europe. The West Highland White Terrier Club of Sweden was founded in 1965.

In many of the countries in Europe it is essential for a dog to have a full mouth if it is to be shown. This means that it must have forty-two teeth or else it is not allowed to be exhibited.

More detailed history

The first breed clubs were formed in Britain in 1905, and since that time the breed has gained great popularity throughout the world.

The ancestors of today's West Highland White Terrier were known by various names such as the Poltalloch, Roseneath or White Scottish Terrier and, to begin with, were kept entirely for their working ability. The breed had to be small and very active in order to follow the quarry to its lair.

As was mentioned in the earlier part of the book, it was found by some to be safer to breed white dogs so that they stood out from the surrounding landscape and were a different colour from their quarry. A painting by Sir Edward Landseer executed in 1839 shows one of these early white terriers. The painting is called *Dignity and Impudence.*

One of the first people to bring the breed into the public eye was Colonel Malcolm of Poltalloch. He had a large kennel of working dogs, loved the breed and thought that they should be better known.

From here the breed started to be developed as a show strain.

The first show to classify separately the West Highland White Terrier was the annual show of the Scottish Kennel Club in October 1904.

At the next Scottish Kennel Club Show in October 1905, Morven won the Championship Certificate and in 1907 became the first champion in the breed. Two other dogs followed in the same year. They were Ch. Cromar Snowflake (by Morven) and Ch. Oronsay.

Between 1907 and 1916 twenty seven Champions were made up and the names of their owners are well known to historians of the breed. Among the owners of these dogs were Miss Viccars (Childwick), Miss Buckley (Scotia), Mrs. B. Lucas (Highclere) and Mrs. C. Pacey (Wolvey) who probably did more for the breed than any one. She became not only a breed judge but one of the best all round judges in the world.

The first of many 'Wolvey' Champions was made up in 1916. This was Ch. Wolvey Piper.

After 1916, all shows were stopped because of the war, and during 1917 and 1918 breeding was prohibited. During this period many dogs had to be destroyed because the food situation was so difficult and some kennels never started again.

Breeding started again slowly in 1919 and the following year shows were restarted. In that year five champions were made up, they were: Ch. Charming of Childwick, Ch. Highclere Rhalet and Ch. Highclere Romp, Ch. Wolvey Skylark and Ch. White Sylph. In the years following; 1920-1939, 125 champions were made up, thirty-two of them being from the Wolvey Kennels.

Between the wars many great kennels were founded and it is difficult in this small space to pay homage to all of them or even to mention them all individually, but even on a pedigree of a well known winner of today, some of these famous affixes may still appear. Names such as Calluna, Wolvey, Rushmoor, Leal and Furzefield all have their place in the history of the breed as well as many more equally famous.

With the resumption of shows in 1946 and all breed championship shows in 1947, came new champions. The first being the bitch Ch. Freshney Fiametta. During the war years many of the good British dogs were sent to America to avoid a repetition of the destruction of the breed, as had happened in the first World War.

Only relatively few of the best dogs were kept by their breeders in this country, one of these being Ch. Melbourne Mathias. After the war he sired Furzefield Piper who is on the pedigree of many of today's show dogs as he was probably the leading stud dog of that time. He was the sire of nine champions, one of the most notable being Ch. Hookwood Mentor who in turn sired eleven champions. His son, Ch. Barrister of Branston, owned by Mrs. Dennis, also sired eleven champions and through these and many other good sons and daughters has left a strong mark on the breed. Dr. & Mrs. Russell's Int. Ch. Cruben Dextor, a son of Mentor, after gaining his title in Britain went to America where he continued to win and sire many champions.

Some of the kennels to the fore in the fifties, sixties and seventies were: Backmuir, Birkfell, Branston, Calluna, Cedarfell, Citrus, Famecheck, Glengyle, Highstile, Incheril, Kendrum, Lasara, Lindenhall, Pillerton, Quakertown, Sollershot, Waideshouse, Whitebriar, Woodpuddle.

During the seventies many new kennels appeared, too numerous to name individually.

One dog must be named here for he was the first and only one of the breed to become Supreme Champion at Cruft's. This was in 1976 and his name is Champion Dianthus Buttons. Bertie, as he is known to his friends, is a good example of a link with the past as he was one of the dogs to be sired by Ch. Alpin of Kendrum in his later years, the sire being born in 1961 and bred by the Hon. T.H. Rollo.

READING LIST

Marvin, John T., *The Complete West Highland Whitc Terrier.* Howell Bk. House Inc.

Dennis, D. Mary, *The West Highland White Terrier.* Popular Dogs Publishing Co. Ltd.

Harmer, Hilary, *Dogs and how to breed them.* John Gifford Limited.

Graham, Capt. R. Portman, *The mating and whelping of dogs.* Popular Dogs Publishing Co. Ltd.

Boorer, Wendy, *Dog Care.* Hamlyn.

Pacey, May, *West Highland White Terriers.* Foyles.

Cartledge, Joe & Liz, *The Complete Illustrated West Highland White Terrier.* Ebury Press.

Hutchinson, Walter, (Editor), *Popular and Illustrated Dog Encyclopaedia.* Hutchinson.

USEFUL ADDRESSES

The Kennel Club, 1 Clarges Street, Piccadilly, London W1Y 8AB, England.

The American Kennel Club, 51 Madison Avenue, New York, N.Y. 10010, USA.

There are many clubs catering for this breed and the addresses of these can be obtained from your Kennel Club.

DOG MAGAZINES

Pure Bred Dogs, American Kennel Gazette, published by the American Kennel Club.

Dog World, 22 New Street, Ashford, Kent, England.

Our Dogs, 5 Oxford Road Station Approach, Manchester 1, England.

Index

Distributors for
Bartholomew Pet Books

Australia

Book Trade: Tudor Distributors Pty. Limited, 14 Mars Road,
Lane Cove 2066, New South Wales, Australia

Canada

Pet Trade: Burgham Sales Ltd., 558 McNicoll Avenue,
Willowdale (Toronto), Ontario, Canada M2H 2E1
Book Trade: Clarke Irwin and Company, Limited,
791 St. Clair Avenue W., Toronto, Canada M6C 1B8

New Zealand

Pet Trade: Masterpet Products Limited,
7 Kaiwharawhara Road, Wellington, New Zealand
Book Trade: Whitcoulls Limited, Trade Department, Private Bag,
Auckland, Wellington, or Christchurch, New Zealand

South Africa

Book Trade: McGraw-Hill Book Company (S.A.) (Pty.) Limited,
P.O. Box 23423, Joubert Park, Johannesburg,
South Africa

U.S.A.

Pet Trade: Pet Supply Imports Inc., P.O. Box 497, Chicago,
Illinois, U.S.A.
Book Trade: The Two Continents Publishing Group Limited,
30 East 42nd Street, New York, N.Y. 10017, U.S.A.